More Praise for
The POETRY *of* IMPERMANENCE,
MINDFULNESS, *and* JOY

"I simply love this anthology of poetry. John Brehm has mined the hearts and minds of forgotten and famous alike, prompting his readers to stretch ever more gently into this ephemeral existence. These poems, ancient and modern, from East and West, point us to a poignant life, where the gateway to meaning involves learning to notice and include the ten thousand joys and sorrows along the way."
—Sarah Powers, author of *Insight Yoga*

"Jubilant, thoughtful, startling, and pure, the poems in *The Poetry of Impermanence, Mindfulness, and Joy* remind us that every poem is a pond, and every pond a poem. Slow down. Dip your toes. See the ripples in each reflected moon. Swim a while in the deep brilliance of language, image, and sound."
—Dinty W. Moore, author of *The Mindful Writer* and director of creative writing, Ohio University

The **POETRY** *of* **IMPERMANENCE,**
MINDFULNESS, *and* **JOY**

edited by John Brehm

Wisdom Publications
132 Perry Street
New York, NY 10014 USA
wisdomexperience.org

Library of Congress Cataloging-in-Publication Data
Names: Brehm, John, 1955– editor.
Title: The poetry of impermanence, mindfulness, and joy / edited by John Brehm.
Description: Boston: Wisdom Publications, [2017]
Identifiers: LCCN 2016044505 (print) | LCCN 2017010221 (ebook) |
    ISBN 9781614293316 (paperback: acid-free paper) | ISBN 1614293317
    (paperback: acid-free paper) | ISBN 9781614293422 (ebook)
Subjects: LCSH: Mindfulness (Psychology)—Poetry. | Impermanence
    (Buddhism)—Poetry. | Dharma (Buddhism)—Poetry. | BISAC: POETRY
    / Inspirational & Religious. | POETRY / Anthologies (multiple authors). |
    RELIGION / Buddhism / General (see also PHILOSOPHY / Buddhist).
Classification: LCC PN6110.M48 P64 2017 (print) | LCC
    PN6110.M48 (ebook) | DDC 808.81/938—dc23
LC record available at https://lccn.loc.gov/2016044505

ISBN 978-1-61429-331-6   ebook ISBN 978-1-61429-342-2

25 24 23   8 7

Cover design by Jim Zaccaria. Cover art: "Our Fragile Past," by Kevin Sloan.
Interior design by Kristin Goble. Set in Adobe Garamond Pro 10.5/14.
Author photo by Cameron Boyd.

Printed in the United States of America.

Please visit fscus.org.

Contents

Introduction. xiii

PART ONE. IMPERMANENCE

Tu Fu, "Jade Flower Palace". 3

Matsuo Bashō, "Summer grasses" 4

Han Shan, "Fields, a house, many mulberry
    trees, fine gardens!" .5

Ryōkan, "I never longed for the wilder side of life". . .6

Saigyō, "'Detached' observer" 7

Robert Frost, "Nothing Gold Can Stay" 8

James Schuyler, "Korean Mums" 9

William Butler Yeats, "The Wild Swans
    at Coole" 12

William Shakespeare, "Sonnet 73". 14

Po Chü-i, "Autumn Thoughts, Sent Far Away". . .15

A. R. Ammons, "Continuing" 16

Saigyō, "Winter has withered everything" 18

Su Tung-P'o, "12th Moon, 14th Sun . . ." 19

Kobayashi Issa, "This world of dew" 20

Kay Ryan, "The Niagara River" 21

Lucia Perillo, "After Reading *The Tibetan Book of the Dead*" 22

William Carlos Williams, "The Widow's Lament in Springtime". 24

Kenneth Rexroth, "Delia Rexroth" 26

Andrea Hollander, "October 9, 1970" 27

Ellen Bass, "If You Knew" 29

William Wordsworth, "A Slumber Did My Spirit Seal" 31

Kobayashi Issa, "Mother I never knew" 32

A. R. Ammons, "In Memoriam Mae Noblitt" . . .33

Frank O'Hara, "The Day Lady Died" 36

Ron Padgett, "Dog". 38

Philip Larkin, "Ambulances" 39

Tomas Tranströmer, "Death stoops over me". . . .41

Yannis Ritsos, "February 23" 42

Ruth Stone, "Train Ride". 43

Czesław Miłosz, "Encounter". 44

Yannis Ritsos, "January 4" 45

Bill Knott, "Death" 46

Pablo Neruda, "Ode to a Dead Carob Tree" 47

Walt Whitman, "Reconciliation" 51

Yusef Komunyakaa, "Facing It" 52

Anna Kamieńska, "I Don't Know How a
    Day Flew by Us" 54

Philip Larkin, "Days" 55

James Schuyler, "The Day" 56

Ikkyū Sojun, "The moon is a house" 58

Eihei Dōgen, "Waka on Impermanence" 59

Yosa Buson, "The old man" 60

Lucia Perillo, "I Could Name Some Names" 61

Han Shan, "They laugh at me,
    'Hey farm boy!'" 63

Jack Kerouac, "In my medicine cabinet" 64

Ron Padgett, "The Joke" 65

PART TWO. MINDFULNESS

Billy Collins, "Shoveling Snow with Buddha" . . . 69

Wallace Stevens, "The Snow Man" 72

Kenneth Rexroth, "Empty Mirror" 73

Gary Snyder, "Piute Creek" 75

Ikkyū Sojun, "After ten years in the
    red-light district" 77

William Stafford, "Listening" 78

Dick Allen, "Listening Deeply" 79

D. H. Lawrence, "The White Horse" 80

A. R. Ammons, "Clarifications" 81

Denise Levertov, "Aware" 82

Anna Swir, "Our Two Silences" 83

Wei Ying-Wu, "In the Depths of
    West Mountain, Visiting the Master" 84

Yosa Buson, "Coolness—" 85

Li Po, "Watching a White Falcon Set Loose" 86

William Carlos Williams, "Fine Work
    with Pitch and Copper" 87

Kobayashi Issa, "The distant mountains" 88

A. R. Ammons, "Reflective" 89

Adam Zagajewski, "Auto Mirror" 90

Robert Frost, "Tree at My Window" 91

Wisława Szymborska, "No Title Required" 92

Bronisław Maj, "A Leaf" 95

Ezra Pound, "In a Station of the Metro" 96

Old Shōju, "One look at plum blossoms" 97

Ron Padgett, "Now You See It" 98

Jane Hirshfield, "Lighthouse" 99

Ikkyū Sojun, "Void in Form" 100

Wallace Stevens, "Study of Two Pears" 101

Elizabeth Bishop, "The Fish" 103

Robert Frost, "Hyla Brook" 107

Shido Bunan, "The moon's the same old moon" 108

Li Po, "Zazen on Ching-t'ing Mountain" 109

Anna Swir, "A Double Rapture". 110

Gary Snyder, "Mid-August at
    Sourdough Mountain Lookout" 111

Eihei Dōgen, "This slowly drifting cloud
    is pitiful" 112

Ryōkan, "The night is fresh and cool" 113

Walt Whitman, "I Stand and Look" 114

Philip Larkin, "Here". 115

Elizabeth Bishop, "Filling Station". 117

William Carlos Williams, "The Poor" 119

Kobayashi Issa, "I'm going to roll over" 121

Wisława Szymborska, "Miracle Fair". 122

Po Chü-i, "Li the Mountain Recluse Stays
    the Night on Our Boat" 124

Matsuo Bashō, "Wrapping the rice cakes" 125

PART THREE. JOY

Ryōkan, "First Days of Spring—the Sky" 129

Su Tung-P'o, "With Mao and Fang,
    Visiting Bright Insight Monastery" 131

Kobayashi Issa, "Children imitating
    cormorants" 132

Ryōkan, "Nothing satisfies some appetites" 133

Chuang-Tzu, "The Joy of Fishes" 134

Han Shan, "The cloud road's choked with
    deep mist. No one gets here that way" 136

Matsuo Bashō, "A field of cotton—" 137

Yosa Buson, "Such a moon—" 138

Kobayashi Issa, "Full moon" 139

Matsuo Bashō, "A cicada shell" 140

James Wright, "A Blessing" 141

Pablo Neruda, "Horses" 143

Jack Gilbert, "Horses at Midnight without
    a Moon" 145

Kobayashi Issa, "Under cherry trees" 146

Tomas Tranströmer, "Face to Face" 147

Marilyn Krysl, "She Speaks a
    Various Language" 148

Saigyō, "Quiet mountain hut" 150

William Stafford, "It's All Right". 151

Jacques Prévert, "The Dunce" 152

Walt Whitman, "When I Heard the Learn'd
    Astronomer" 153

Yosa Buson, "My arm for a pillow" 154

Po Chü-i, "After *Quiet Joys at South Garden*
    Sent by P'ei Tu". 155

William Stafford, "Ask Me". 156

Pablo Neruda, "Ode to My Socks". 157

Ron Padgett, "Inaction of Shoes". 161

Anna Swir, "Priceless Gifts". 162

Yannis Ritsos, "January 21" 163

A. R. Ammons, "Stills" 164

Han Shan, "My old landlady" 165

Fernando Pessoa, "Calm because
    I'm unknown". 166

Tracy K. Smith, "Credulity" 167

Billy Collins, "Aimless Love" 168

Jack Gilbert, "A Brief for the Defense". 170

A. R. Ammons, "The City Limits". 172

Marianne Moore, "What Are Years?". 174

Alicia Ostriker, "Wrinkly Lady Dancer" 176

William Carlos Williams, "To Waken
  an Old Lady"............................177

Jack Gilbert, "Getting Old"................178

Ron Padgett, "Words from the Front".........180

Paulann Petersen, "Why the Aging Poet
  Continues to Write" 181

A. R. Ammons, "Old Geezer" 182

Ryōkan, "Don't say my hut has nothing
  to offer"...............................183

APPENDICES

Mindful Reading..........................187

Meditation on Sounds 193

Biographical Notes........................197

Credits..................................257

Acknowledgments 277

About the Editor 279

Introduction

No poem can last for long unless it speaks, even if obliquely, to some essential human concern. Tu Fu's poem about the pathos of ruins at Jade Flower Palace, which opens this anthology, has lasted more than thirteen centuries, reminding us that impermanence is one of poetry's oldest themes, perhaps *the* oldest. Of the prince who ruled there long ago, Tu Fu writes:

> *His dancing girls are yellow dust.*
> *Their painted cheeks have crumbled*
> *Away. His gold chariots*
> *and courtiers are gone. Only*
> *A stone horse is left of his*
> *Glory.*

Awareness of the fleeting nature of things may well have sparked the first poetic utterance. Lewis Mumford in *The History of the City* suggests that the earliest human settlements arose when our distant hunter-gatherer ancestors refused to leave their dead behind. It's not hard to imagine that such a decision may also have inspired elegiac honoring of the dead in the form of heightened speech or songlike lament, a kind of protopoetry.

Ki no Tsurayuki in his preface to *Kokin Wakashū*, the first imperially sponsored anthology of *waka* poetry, published in 905, observed:

> When these poets saw the scattered spring blossoms, when they heard leaves falling in the autumn evening, when they saw reflected in their mirrors the snow and the waves of each passing year, when they were stunned into an awareness of the brevity of life by the dew on the grass or foam on the water . . . they were inspired to write poems.

"Death is the mother of beauty," as Wallace Stevens would put it a thousand years later. There are other sources of inspiration, of course, but none more ancient or enduring than the pang that accompanies our experience of loss—and our uniquely human foreknowledge of loss.

Perhaps there is some comfort in knowing that impermanence defies its own law, is exempt from its own implacable strictures, is itself unchanging. Ikkyū states the paradox succinctly: "Only impermanence lasts." The truth of impermanence, as Ryōkan says, is "a timeless truth." It is not historically or culturally conditioned. It is not an idea but a process, observable anywhere at any time. Buddhist poets of ancient China and Japan may have been more finely attuned to that truth, through formal meditation practice, but Western poets are held within the law of impermanence no less firmly than their Asian counterparts, and awareness that all things pass away is inescapable for anyone who pays attention. Of course, our culture encourages us *not* to pay attention, to live as if we will live forever, as if we can plunder the earth unceasingly and without consequence. "What dreamwalkers men become," Master Dōgen writes.

But living in alignment with the truth of impermanence opens a secret passageway to joy. Once we acknowledge how inherently unstable are the pleasures of "this floating world," we are free to love all things without attachment. In *The Trauma of Everyday Life,* the Buddhist psychotherapist Mark Epstein tells a story about asking the great Thai Forest monk Ajahn Chah to explain the Buddhist view. Chah held up a glass of water and said:

I love this glass. It holds the water admirably. When the sun shines on it, it reflects the light beautifully. When I tap it, it has a lovely ring. Yet for me, this glass is already broken. When the wind knocks it over or my elbow knocks it off the shelf and it falls to the ground and shatters, I say, "Of course." But when I understand that this glass is already broken, every minute with it is precious.

It is only our quite natural but completely impossible expectation that conditions remain stable that makes sudden changes sting as much as they do. If we knew ourselves as living in a ghost world of unceasing change, we wouldn't take ourselves and the things that happen to us quite so seriously. And we would see more clearly the preciousness of all life. Ellen Bass asks the provocative question, "What if you knew you'd be the last / to touch someone?"

> What would people look like
> if we could see them as they are,
> soaked in honey, stung and swollen,
> reckless, pinned against time?

In the closing couplet of "Sonnet 73," Shakespeare writes, "This thou perceiv'st, which makes thy love more strong, / To love that well which thou must leave ere long." Yamamoto Tsunetomo, in the eighteenth-century samurai manual *Hagakure*, takes this idea of *already broken* or *soon gone* a step further, advising us to meditate on inevitable death every day: "If by setting one's heart right every morning and evening, one is able to live as though his body were already dead, he gains freedom in the Way."

Ajahn Chah and Tsunetomo make explicit the underlying premise of this anthology: that mindfulness of impermanence leads to joy. Living in the full knowledge that everything changes changes everything. It loosens our grasp and lets the world become what it truly is, a source of amazement and amusement. Han Shan says:

> Once you realize this floating life is the perfect
>   mirage of change,
> it's breathtaking—this wild joy at wandering
>   boundless and free.

Freedom from craving and from fixed ideas of self lets us experience the world as a friendly place where, as in Ron Padgett's "Inaction of Shoes," the things we have to do thank us for doing them; or like Chuang-Tzu we know the joy of fishes, and all other beings, through our own joy; or with Ryōkan we "pretend to be a crane softly floating among the clouds." When we let go of insisting that we are who we think we are and that the world should give us exactly and only what we want, all things shine forth. A pair of wool socks, knitted "with threads of dusk and sheep's wool," becomes perfectly miraculous in Pablo Neruda's "Ode to My Socks"; a "pretty bubble in your soup at noon" banishes despair in William Stafford's "It's All Right"; and a caged bird singing in Marianne Moore's "What Are Years?" lets us know that "satisfaction is a lowly / thing, how pure a thing is joy."

Moore, though hardly a Buddhist, illuminates an essential aspect of the Buddha's teachings: the difference between satisfying a desire and being *released* from desire, which is the difference between pleasure and peace. But we are conditioned to prefer pleasure, and to pursue it relentlessly, rather than to relax into joy.

The poems gathered here point to a different way of being in the world, and they do so in part by inverting conventional valuations. When Ryōkan, on his daily rounds of alms gathering, is hijacked by the village children, he happily puts aside his begging bowl and joins in their singsongs and kick-ball. And when his behavior arouses the scorn of more practical-minded adults, Ryōkan asserts the deep power and absolute rightness of his joy:

> I kick the ball and they sing, they kick and I
>   sing.
> Time is forgotten, the hours fly.
> People passing by point at me and laugh:
> "Why are you acting like such a fool?"
> I nod my head and don't answer.
> I could say something, but why?
> Do you want to know what's in my heart?
> From the beginning of time: just this! just this!

He does not bother replying to the people who ridi-cule him, but he does tell *us* where joy can be found: in the present moment. Indeed, Ryōkan's "just this!" is Zen in a nutshell—just this moment, nothing added, pure consciousness stripped clean of all our self-centered stories and desires. The people who pass by are caught up in reaction, judgment, aversion, just as we all are. But Ryōkan does not judge them. The poem wonderfully dramatizes two ways of being—one that is childlike, spontaneous, open to sudden delight; the other rigid, reactive, always with better things to do than play with children or act like a fool.

Many of the poems in *The Poetry of Impermanence, Mindfulness, and Joy* have this subtly subversive quality. Issa gently undermines our human arrogance, placing himself on equal footing with all other beings, even insects:

> *I'm going to roll over,*
> *so please move,*
>   *cricket.*

Likewise, in "Ode to a Dead Carob Tree," Pablo Neruda feels an immediate kinship with a fallen tree. He is on his way elsewhere, but the tree stops him, he lets it stop him, just as Ryōkan lets the children interrupt his alms-gathering and Issa pauses to give the cricket time to move. This act of stopping and attending mindfully to what the present moment presents is crucial:

> *I walked closer, and such*
> *was its ruined strength,*
> *so heroic the branches on the ground,*
> *the crown radiating such*
> *earthly majesty,*
> *that when*
> *I touched its trunk*
> *I felt it throbbing,*

and a surge
from the heart of the tree
made me close my eyes
and bow
my head.

In a sustained act of seeing, Neruda takes it all in, the fallen carob tree's physical form, its roots "twisted / like tangled hair," but also its kingly spirit—its "heroic branches on the ground," its crown that radiates an "earthly majesty." Seeing the tree in this way, *being* with it, leads to an act of empathic connection: he *touches* the tree. It is this physical contact that allows Neruda to experience "a surge / from the heart of the tree." Notice how easily he says "the heart of the tree" and how easily we accept it, remembering for a moment what we have learned to forget—that all things are animated by the same life force that animates us, that all things are our brothers and sisters. And then Neruda closes his eyes and bows his head in an ancient gesture of vulnerability and reverence. It's the same impulse that compels Whitman in "Reconciliation," a poem written just after the end of the Civil War, to bend down and place a kiss on the face of his "enemy," a Confederate soldier:

For my enemy is dead—a man divine as myself
    is dead;
I look where he lies, white-faced and still in the
    coffin—I draw near;
I bend down, and touch lightly with my lips the
    white face in the coffin.

In "No Title Required," Wisława Szymborska catalogues a series of events typically considered significant—great battles, coronations, revolutions—alongside "ordinary" things—clouds passing, a river flowing by, grass stitched into the ground, and concludes:

So it happens that I am and look.
Above me a white butterfly is fluttering through
    the air
on wings that are its alone,

and a shadow skims through my hands
that is none other than itself, no one else's but
    its own.

When I see such things, I'm no longer sure
that what's important
is more important than what's not.

"So it happens that I am and look" might be the banner that hangs over this book. That act of mindful attending is essential to these poems. Old Shōju says, "Want 'meaningless' Zen? / Just look— at anything!" And Li Po shows that such looking dissolves the sense of separateness that plagues us and that even Einstein regarded as a kind of optical delusion.

> *The birds have vanished down the sky.*
> *Now the last cloud drains away.*
>
> *We sit together, the mountain and me,*
> *until only the mountain remains.*

This kind of seeing requires mindfulness—the intentional, nonjudging awareness of present-moment experience. In my own practice of neighborhood walking meditation I have found that looking intently, without judgment, at the most "insignificant" things—hubcaps, weathered fence posts, gate latches, bolts on fire hydrants, weeds, trash on the street, and so on—has the most profoundly awakening effect.

Just as impermanence calls us to be mindful, the practice of mindfulness heightens our awareness of impermanence. Following moment-to-moment experience in meditation reveals the fluid condition of all we perceive. The breath arises and falls away, sounds appear and disappear, bodily sensations vibrate in one spot and then another, thoughts leapfrog over each other and are gone—everything changing, coming into form, and slipping into formlessness again. In the external world it is no different. A stone may occupy reality longer than a fruit fly or a thought, but a difference in duration is not a difference in destination or destiny. In time, the thought, the fly, and the stone all arrive at the same place.

～

I felt the full force of impermanence in my own life in 2009, when my nephew George was suddenly hospitalized in Japan—he was half-Japanese—where he had been teaching English. Though he didn't know it at the time, he suffered from an extremely rare liver disease, porphyria, which sent him into liver failure. In the space of two weeks, he went from living a healthy and active life—he had just gotten engaged and was flourishing as a teacher—to being on the brink of death. A liver transplant was the only possibility of saving him. Because I was the only viable donor in our family, I immediately flew to Kyoto to undergo a transplant that would give half my liver to George. The operation itself was successful, but George suffered a massive brain hemorrhage two days later and did not survive. He had just turned twenty-eight. His death was a devastation for all who knew him.

That he died in Kyoto was especially poignant, because George and I shared a love for the poet Saigyō, who had lived in Kyoto in the twelfth century. Like me, George read and wrote poetry (the only other person in my family to share that passion), and I had brought books by Neruda and Saigyō with me, imagining we would read poems together as we recovered from the surgery.

I had to remain in Kyoto for a month of follow-up treatment, and though I was hobbled and grieving, I was able to visit some of the city's ancient Buddhist temples and to walk some of the same cobblestone lanes where Saigyō, Dōgen, Bashō, Ikkyū, Buson, and so many other great poets had perhaps walked. The experience of losing my nephew in a city that has been for centuries a wellspring of poetry and Zen planted the seeds for what would become *The Poetry of Impermanence, Mindfulness, and Joy.*

Ananda, the beloved disciple of the Buddha, once asked, "Master, are good spiritual friends fully half of the holy life?" "No, Ananda," the Buddha replied. "Good spiritual friends are the *whole* of the holy life." The poems gathered here feel like spiritual friends. They offer everything one might hope for in a such a friendship: wisdom, compassion, peacefulness, clear seeing, good humor, and the ability to both absorb and express the deepest human emotions of grief, loss, and joy. And if the poems feel like friends, the book itself may come to seem like a poetic sangha, a remarkable—and portable—spiritual community spanning more than two millennia and ranging from Anna Swir to A. R. Ammons, Chuang-Tzu to Czesław Miłosz, Saigyō to Gary Snyder, and many others ancient and modern, Eastern and Western, Buddhist and non-Buddhist.

One of my goals in gathering these poems has been to show how beautifully the Dharma manifests even in poems by poets who were not practicing Buddhists or knew little or nothing about Buddhism. The term *dharma* has a complex etymology, but in current usage it has two main meanings. It refers to teachings of the Buddha, and more broadly to the way things are, universal law, or the truth of things. It is in this latter sense that I'm using the term. These poems show us the truth of things.

The Poetry of Impermanence, Mindfulness, and Joy is not intended to be definitive. These are simply the poems I've found most powerful on these three themes. Many of them have been friends for years, poems that I have returned to again and again, taken comfort in and been astonished by—poems that have deepened my spiritual practice and helped me feel alive to the wonder and strangeness and sadness of the world. Many others are new discoveries that came to me as the anthology began to take shape, as I read more deeply in ancient Chinese and Japanese poetry, and as I began to see the Dharma suddenly lit up in many modern, non-Buddhist poems. The result is an extremely personal, nonscholarly (but I hope not eccentric) selection. I have also left out some poets one might expect to find in an anthology of this kind. Another of my goals has been to give Dharma teachers and students a broader spectrum of poetry to draw upon, beyond the widely popular poems of Rumi, Hafiz, and Mary Oliver, and to introduce them to poems and poets they might not otherwise encounter.

Deciding how to organize the book often felt very much like arranging stanzas in a poem—and in a sense, each of the sections, and the book in its entirety, can be read as a single poem in many voices. I've grouped the poems by affinity and resonance rather than chronology or nationality, and every poem is connected to and colored by the poems that immediately surround it. The book invites random browsing, but reading the poems in sequence may be more rewarding.

My wish is that these poems may become spiritual companions on your path, deepen your practice, whatever it might be, and offer a taste of that eternally transient delight that is always disappearing and always present.

PART ONE

Impermanence

Tu Fu
712–770

Jade Flower Palace

The stream swirls. The wind moans in
The pines. Grey rats scurry over
Broken tiles. What prince, long ago,
Built this palace, standing in
Ruins beside the cliffs? There are
Green ghost fires in the black rooms.
The shattered pavements are all
Washed away. Ten thousand organ
Pipes whistle and roar. The storm
Scatters the red autumn leaves.
His dancing girls are yellow dust.
Their painted cheeks have crumbled
Away. His gold chariots
and courtiers are gone. Only
A stone horse is left of his
Glory. I sit on the grass and
Start a poem, but the pathos of
It overcomes me. The future
Slips imperceptibly away.
Who can say what the years will bring?

Translated from the Chinese by Kenneth Rexroth.

Matsuo Bashō

1644–1694

summer grasses—
all that remains
of warriors' dreams

Translated from the Japanese by Lucien Stryk and Takashi Ikemoto.

Han Shan

Ninth century

Fields, a house, many mulberry trees, fine gardens!
Oxen and calves fill his stables and his
    well-trodden roads.
He knows for sure from all this that all effects
    have causes,
and that only fools buy early and sell late.
So his eyes can see too how it could all get gone,
ground down, melted, all away . . .
These things can knock on the heads of everyone
    living,
like the Abbot's knock on the noggin of the errant
    novice.
You can end up in paper pants, or worse, with
a broken tile, pierced and hung on a thong
flip-flapping over your private parts . . .
and sure as sure, you'll end up dead,
maybe starved or frozen, but certainly dead.

Translated from the Chinese by J. P. Seaton.

Ryōkan

1758–1831

I never longed for the wilder side of life.
Rivers and mountains were my friends.

Clouds consumed my shadow where I roamed,
and birds pass high above my resting place.

Straw sandals in snowy villages,
a walking stick in spring,

I sought a timeless truth: the flower's glory
is just another form of dust.

Translated from the Japanese by Sam Hamill.

Saigyō

1118–1190

"Detached" observer
of blossoms finds himself in time
intimate with them—
so, when they separate from the branch,
it's he who falls . . . deeply into grief.

Translated from the Japanese by William LeFleur.

Robert Frost

1874–1963

Nothing Gold Can Stay

Nature's first green is gold,
Her hardest hue to hold.
Her early leaf's a flower;
But only so an hour.
Then leaf subsides to leaf.
So Eden sank to grief,
So dawn goes down to day.
Nothing gold can stay.

James Schuyler

1923–1991

Korean Mums

Beside me in this garden
are huge and daisy-like
(why not? are not
oxeye daisies a chrysanthemum?),
shrubby and thick-stalked,
the leaves pointing up
the stems from which
the flowers burst in
sunbursts. I love
this garden in all its moods,
even under its winter coat
of salt hay, or now,
in October, more than
half gone over: here
a rose, there a clump
of aconite. This morning
one of the dogs killed
a barn owl. Bob saw
it happen, tried to
intervene. The airedale
snapped its neck and left

it lying. Now the bird
lies buried by an apple
tree. Last evening
from the table we saw
the owl, huge in the dusk,
circling the field
on owl-silent wings.
The first one ever seen
here: now it's gone,
a dream you just remember.

The dogs are barking. In
the studio music plays
and Bob and Darragh paint.
I sit scribbling in a little
notebook at a garden table,
too hot in a heavy shirt
in the mid-October sun
into which the Korean mums
all face. There is a
dull book with me,
an apple core, cigarettes,
an ashtray. Behind me
the rue I gave Bob
flourishes. Light on leaves,
so much to see, and

all I really see is that
owl, its bulk troubling
the twilight. I'll
soon forget it: what
is there I have not forgot?
Or one day will forget:
this garden, the breeze
in stillness, even
the words, Korean mums.

William Butler Yeats

1865–1939

The Wild Swans at Coole

The trees are in their autumn beauty,
The woodland paths are dry,
Under the October twilight the water
Mirrors a still sky;
Upon the brimming water among the stones
Are nine and fifty swans.

The nineteenth Autumn has come upon me
Since I first made my count;
I saw, before I had well finished,
All suddenly mount
And scatter wheeling in great broken rings
Upon their clamorous wings.

I have looked upon those brilliant creatures,
And now my heart is sore.
All's changed since I, hearing at twilight,
The first time on this shore,
The bell-beat of their wings above my head,
Trod with a lighter tread.

Unwearied still, lover by lover,
They paddle in the cold,
Companionable streams or climb the air;
Their hearts have not grown old;
Passion or conquest, wander where they will,
Attend upon them still.

But now they drift on the still water,
Mysterious, beautiful;
Among what rushes will they build,
By what lake's edge or pool
Delight men's eyes, when I awake some day
To find they have flown away?

William Shakespeare

1564–1616

Sonnet 73

That time of year thou mayst in me behold
When yellow leaves, or none, or few, do hang
Upon those boughs which shake against the cold,
Bare ruin'd choirs, where late the sweet birds sang.
In me thou see'st the twilight of such day
As after sunset fadeth in the west;
Which by and by black night doth take away,
Death's second self, that seals up all in rest.
In me thou see'st the glowing of such fire,
That on the ashes of his youth doth lie,
As the death-bed whereon it must expire,
Consum'd with that which it was nourish'd by.
This thou perceiv'st, which makes thy love
    more strong,
To love that well which thou must leave ere long.

Po Chü-i
772–846

Autumn Thoughts, Sent Far Away

We share all these disappointments of failing
autumn a thousand miles apart. This is where

autumn wind easily plunders courtyard trees,
but the sorrows of distance never scatter away.

Swallow shadows shake out homeward wings.
Orchid scents thin, drifting from old thickets.

These lovely seasons and fragrant years falling
lonely away—we share such emptiness here.

Translated from the Chinese by David Hinton.

A. R. Ammons

1926–2001

Continuing

Continuing the show, some prize-winning
leaves broad and firm, a good year,
I checked the ground
for the accumulation of
fifty seasons: last year was
prominent to notice, whole leaves
curled, some still with color:
and, underneath, the year
before, though paler, had structure,
partial, airier than linen:
but under that,
sand or rocksoil already mixed
with the meal or grist:
is this, I said to the mountain,
what becomes of things:
well, the mountain said, one
mourns the dead but who
can mourn those the dead mourned;
back a way
they sift in a tearless
place: but, I said,

it's so quick, don't you think,
quick: most time, the mountain said, lies
in the thinnest layer: who
could bear to hear of it:
I scooped up the sand which flowed
away, all but a cone in the palm:
the mountain said, it
will do for another year.

Saigyō

1118–1190

Winter has withered everything
in this cold mountain place:
dignity is in
its desolation now, and beauty
in the cold clarity of its moon.

Translated from the Japanese by William LeFleur.

Su Tung-P'o
1037–1101

12th Moon, 14th Sun: A Light Snow Fell Overnight, So I Set Out Early for South Creek, Stopped for a Quick Meal and Arrived Late

Snowfall at South Creek: it's the most priceless
    of things,
so I set out to see it before it melts. Hurrying
    my horse,

pushing through thickets alone, I watch for
    footprints,
and at dawn, I'm first across fresh snow on a red
    bridge!

Houses in shambles beyond belief, nowhere even
    to sleep,
I sit facing a village of starvation, voices
    mere murmurs.

Only the evening crows know my thoughts,
    startled into
flight, a thousand flakes tumbling through
    cold branches.

Translated from the Chinese by David Hinton.

Kobayashi Issa

1763–1828

This world of dew
is only the world of dew—
and yet . . . oh and yet . . .

Translated from the Japanese by Robert Hass.

Kay Ryan
1945–

The Niagara River

As though
the river were
a floor, we position
our table and chairs
upon it, eat, and
have conversation.
As it moves along,
we notice—as
calmly as though
dining room paintings
were being replaced—
the changing scenes
along the shore. We
do know, we do
know this is the
Niagara River, but
it is hard to remember
what that means.

Lucia Perillo

1958–2016

After Reading *The Tibetan Book of the Dead*

The hungry ghosts are ghosts whose throats
stretch for miles, a pinprick wide,
so they can drink and drink and are never sated.
Every grain of sand is gargantuan
and water goes down thick as bile.

I don't know how many births it takes to get
reborn as not the flower but the scent.
To be allowed to exist as air (a prayer
to whom?)—dear whom:
the weight of being is too much.

Victor Feguer, for his final meal,
asked for an olive with a pit
so that a tree might sprout from him.
It went down hard, but now the murderer is
     comfort.
He is a shady spot in the potter's field.

But it might be painful to be a tree,
to stand so long with your arms up.

You might prefer to be a rock
(if you can wear that heavy cloak).
In Bamiyan, the limestone Buddhas stood

as tall as minor mountains, each one carved
in its own alcove. When their heads
eroded over time, the swallows
built nests from their dust,
even after zealots blew them up.

Now the swallows wheel in empty alcoves,
their mouths full of ancient rubble.
Each hungry ghost hawks up his pebble
so he can breathe. And the dead
multiply under the olive tree.

William Carlos Williams

1883–1963

The Widow's Lament in Springtime

Sorrow is my own yard
where the new grass
flames as it has flamed
often before but not
with the cold fire
that closes round me this year.
Thirty-five years
I lived with my husband.
The plum tree is white today
with masses of flowers.
Masses of flowers
load the cherry branches
and color some bushes
yellow and some red
but the grief in my heart
is stronger than they
for though they were my joy
formerly, today I notice them
and turn away forgetting.
Today my son told me
that in the meadows,

at the edge of the heavy woods
in the distance, he saw
trees of white flowers.
I feel that I would like
to go there
and fall into those flowers
and sink into the marsh near them.

Kenneth Rexroth
1905–1982

Delia Rexroth
Died June, 1916

Under your illkempt yellow roses,
Delia, today you are younger
Than your son. Two and a half decades—
The family monument sagged askew,
And he overtook your half-a-life.
On the other side of the country,
Near the willows by the slow river,
Deep in the earth, the white ribs retain
The curve of your fervent, careful breast;
The fine skull, the ardor of your brain.
And in the fingers the memory
Of Chopin études, and in the feet
Slow waltzes and champagne two-steps sleep.
And the white full moon of midsummer,
That you watched awake all that last night,
Watches history fill the deserts
And oceans with corpses once again;
And looks in the east window at me,
As I move past you to middle age
And knowledge past your agony and waste.

Andrea Hollander

1947–

October 9, 1970

The same automatic doors
and the same white-haired volunteer,
the elevator and the corridor
with its antiseptic odor
and hushed voices
door after door
down one more hall and again
through the double doors—
but this morning
the lone nurse standing
before the door of 246,
and immediately inside,
the view through the window
of the other wing,
its dozens of identical windows,
and here the pale green walls
paler today behind the blank
screen of the TV
protruding from the wall
and on the movable
metal bedside table

the familiar plastic glass of water
with its bent straw
peering out like a periscope
through its plastic lid
as if only a hidden eye
had full view of the bed
and the body of the woman in it
who was once my mother.

Ellen Bass

1947–

If You Knew

What if you knew you'd be the last
to touch someone?
If you were taking tickets, for example,
at the theater, tearing them,
giving back the ragged stubs,
you might take care to touch that palm,
brush your fingertips
along the life line's crease.

When a man pulls his wheeled suitcase
too slowly through the airport, when
the car in front of me doesn't signal,
when the clerk at the pharmacy
won't say *Thank you*, I don't remember
they're going to die.

A friend told me she'd been with her aunt.
They'd just had lunch and the waiter,
a young gay man with plum black eyes,
joked as he served the coffee, kissed
her aunt's powdered cheek when they left.

Then they walked half a block and her aunt
dropped dead on the sidewalk.

How close does the dragon's spume
have to come? How wide does the crack
in heaven have to split?
What would people look like
if we could see them as they are,
soaked in honey, stung and swollen,
reckless, pinned against time?

William Wordsworth

1770–1850

A Slumber Did My Spirit Seal

A slumber did my spirit seal;
I had no human fears:
She seemed a thing that could not feel
The touch of earthly years.

No motion has she now, no force;
She neither hears nor sees;
Rolled round in earth's diurnal course,
With rocks, and stones, and trees.

Kobayashi Issa

1763–1828

Mother I never knew,
every time I see the ocean,
every time—

Translated from the Japanese by Robert Hass.

A. R. Ammons
1926–2001

In Memoriam Mae Noblitt

This is just a place:
we go around, distanced,
yearly in a star's

atmosphere, turning
daily into and out of
direct light and

slanting through the
quadrant seasons: deep
space begins at our

heels, nearly rousing
us loose: we look up
or out so high, sight's

silk almost draws us away:
this is just a place:
currents worry themselves

coiled and free in airs
and oceans: water picks
up mineral shadow and

plasm into billions of
designs, frames: trees,
grains, bacteria: but

is love a reality we
made here ourselves—
and grief—did we design

that—or do these,
like currents, whine
in and out among us merely

as we arrive and go:
this is just a place:
the reality we agree with,

that agrees with us,
outbounding this, arrives
to touch, joining with

us from far away:
our home which defines
us is elsewhere but not

so far away we have
forgotten it:
this is just a place.

Frank O'Hara

1926–1966

The Day Lady Died

It is 12:20 in New York a Friday
three days after Bastille Day, yes
it is 1959, and I go get a shoeshine
because I will get off the 4:19 in East Hampton
at 7:15 and then go straight to dinner
and I don't know the people who will feed me

I walk up the muggy street beginning to sun
and have a hamburger and a malted and buy
an ugly NEW WORLD WRITING to see what the poets
in Ghana are doing these days
                       I go on to the bank
and Miss Stillwagon (first name Linda I once
    heard)
doesn't even look up my balance for once in her life
and in the GOLDEN GRIFFEN I get a little Verlaine
for Patsy with drawings by Bonnard although I do
think of Hesiod, trans. Richmond Lattimore or
Brendan Behan's new play or Le Balcon or Les
    Nègres

of Genet, but I don't, I stick with Verlaine
after practically going to sleep with quandariness

and for Mike I just stroll into the PARK LANE
Liquor Store and ask for a bottle of Strega, and
then I go back where I came from to 6th Avenue
and the tobacconist in the Ziegfeld Theatre and
casually ask for a carton of Gauloises and a carton
of Picayunes, and a NEW YORK POST with her face
        on it

and I am sweating a lot by now and thinking of
leaning on the john door in the 5 SPOT
while she whispered a song along the keyboard
to Mal Waldron and everyone and I stopped
        breathing.

Ron Padgett

1942–

Dog

The New York streets look nude and stupid
With Ted and Edwin no longer here
To light them up with their particularity
Of loving them and with intelligence
In some large sense of the word:
New York's lost some of its rough charm
And there's just no getting around it
By pretending the rest of us can somehow make up
    for it
Or that future generations will. I hear
A dog barking in the street and it's drizzling
At 6 A.M. and there's nothing warm
Or lovable or necessary about it, it's just
Some dog barking in some street somewhere.
I hate that dog.

Philip Larkin

1922–1985

Ambulances

Closed like confessionals, they thread
Loud noons of cities, giving back
None of the glances they absorb.
Light glossy grey, arms on a plaque.
They come to rest at any kerb:
All streets in time are visited.

Then children strewn on steps or road,
Or women coming from the shops
Past smells of different dinners, see
A wild white face that overtops
Red stretcher-blankets momently
As it is carried in and stowed,

And sense the solving emptiness
That lies just under all we do,
And for a second get it whole,
So permanent and blank and true.
The fastened doors recede. Poor soul,
They whisper at their own distress;

For borne away in deadened air
May go the sudden shut of loss
Round something nearly at an end,
And what cohered in it across
The years, the unique random blend
Of families and fashions, there

At last begin to loosen. Far
From the exchange of love to lie
Unreachable inside a room
The traffic parts to let go by
Brings closer what is left to come,
And dulls to distance all we are.

Tomas Tranströmer

1931–2015

Death stoops over me.
I'm a problem in chess. He
has the solution.

Translated from the Swedish by Robin Fulton.

Yannis Ritsos

1909–1990

February 23

The moon white
drum-tight
like the belly of the drowned.

Manolis used to say:
everything's going to be fine.
His heart said so.

Manolis
down in the deep water
with the blind seaweed.

Translated from the Greek by Edmund Keeley and Karen Emmerich.

Ruth Stone

1915–2011

Train Ride

All things come to an end;
small calves in Arkansas,
the bend of the muddy river.
Do all things come to an end?
No, they go on forever.
They go on forever, the swamp,
the vine-choked cypress, the oaks
rattling last year's leaves,
the thump of the rails, the kite,
the still white stilted heron.
All things come to an end.
The red clay bank, the spread hawk,
the bodies riding this train,
the stalled truck, pale sunlight, the talk;
the talk goes on forever,
the wide dry field of geese,
a man stopped near his porch
to watch. Release, release;
between cold death and a fever,
send what you will, I will listen.
All things come to an end.
No, they go on forever.

Czesław Miłosz

1911–2004

Encounter

We were riding through frozen fields in a wagon
    at dawn.
A red wing rose in the darkness.

And suddenly a hare ran across the road.
One of us pointed to it with his hand.

That was long ago. Today neither of them is alive,
Not the hare, nor the man who made the gesture.

O my love, where are they, where are they going.
The flash of a hand, streak of movement, rustle
    of pebbles.
I ask not out of sorrow, but in wonder.

Translated from the Polish by Robert Hass and the author.

Yannis Ritsos

1909–1990

January 4

And suddenly
a memory of birds
that sank into the unknown.

Translated from the Greek by Edmund Keeley and Karen Emmerich.

Bill Knott

1940–2014

Death

Going to sleep, I cross my hands on my chest.
They will place my hands like this.
It will look as though I am flying into myself.

Pablo Neruda

1904–1973

Ode to a Dead Carob Tree

We were traveling from
Totoral, dusty
was our planet,
pampa encircled
by azure sky:
heat and light in emptiness.
It was
passing through
Yaco Barranca
toward forsaken Ongamira
that we saw
horizontal on the prairie
a toppled giant,
a dead carob tree.

Last night's
storm
ripped out its silvery
roots,
left them twisted
like tangled hair, a tortured mane

unmoving in the wind.
I walked closer, and such
was its ruined strength,
so heroic the branches on the ground,
the crown radiating such
earthly majesty,
that when
I touched its trunk
I felt it throbbing,
and a surge
from the heart of the tree
made me close my eyes
and bow
my head.

It was sturdy and furrowed
by time, a strong
column carved
by earth and rain,
and like a
candelabrum
it had spread its rounded
arms of wood
to lavish
green light and shadow
on the plain.

The American
storm, the
blue
north wind
of the prairie,
had overtaken
this sturdy carob,
goblet
strong as iron,
and with a blast from the sky
had felled its beauty.

I stood there staring
at what only yesterday
had harbored
forest sounds and nests,
but I did not weep
because my dead brother
was as beautiful in death as in life.

I said good-bye. And left it
lying there
on the mother earth.

I left the wind
keeping watch and weeping,

and from afar I saw
the
wind
caressing its head.

Translated from the Spanish by Margaret Sayers Peden.

Walt Whitman

1819–1892

Reconciliation

Word over all, beautiful as the sky!
Beautiful that war, and all its deeds of carnage,
    must in time be utterly lost;
That the hands of the sisters Death and Night,
    incessantly softly wash again,
    and ever again, this soil'd world:
For my enemy is dead—a man divine as myself is
    dead;
I look where he lies, white-faced and still, in the
    coffin—I draw near;
I bend down, and touch lightly with my lips the
    white face in the coffin.

Yusef Komunyakaa

1947–

Facing It

My black face fades,
hiding inside the black granite.
I said I wouldn't,
dammit: No tears.
I'm stone. I'm flesh.
My clouded reflection eyes me
like a bird of prey, the profile of night
slanted against morning. I turn
this way—the stone lets me go.
I turn that way—I'm inside
the Vietnam Veterans Memorial
again, depending on the light
to make a difference.
I go down the 58,022 names,
half-expecting to find
my own in letters like smoke.
I touch the name Andrew Johnson;
I see the booby trap's white flash.
Names shimmer on a woman's blouse
but when she walks away
the names stay on the wall.

Brushstrokes flash, a red bird's
wings cutting across my stare.
The sky. A plane in the sky.
A white vet's image floats
closer to me, then his pale eyes
look through mine. I'm a window.
He's lost his right arm
inside the stone. In the black mirror
a woman's trying to erase names:
No, she's brushing a boy's hair.

Anna Kamieńska

1920–1986

I Don't Know How a Day Flew By Us

I don't know how a day flew by us
I don't know how life flew by us
and closed with a word
like a lake with ice
winter passed snows melted
the suns appeared and saw
after the winter
that scar on the earth
your grave

Translated from the Polish by David Curzon and Grazyna Drabik.

Philip Larkin
1922–1985

Days

What are days for?
Days are where we live.
They come, they wake us
Time and time over.
They are to be happy in:
Where can we live but days?

Ah, solving that question
Brings the priest and the doctor
In their long coats
Running over the fields.

James Schuyler

1923–1991

The Day

The day is gray
as stone: the stones
embedded in the
dirt road are chips
of it. How dark it
gets here in the
north when a cold
front moves in. The
wind starts up. It
keens around the
house in long
sharp sighs at
windows. More
leaves come down
and are borne
sidewise. In the
woods a flock
of small white
moths fluttered,
flying, like the
leaves. The wind

in trees, a
heavy surge, drowns
out the water-
fall: from here,
a twisted thread.
Winter knocks at
the door. Don't
let it in. But
those shivering,
hovering, late
moths,
the size of big
snowflakes: what
were they doing
there, so late
in the year? Had
they laid their
eggs, and fluttered
in the then still
woods, aware of
the coming wind,
the storm, their
end? But they
were beautiful,
there in the woods,
frantic with life.

Ikkyū Sojun

1394–1481

The moon is a house
in which the mind is master.
Look very closely:
only impermanence lasts.
The floating world, too, will pass.

Translated from the Japanese by Sam Hamill.

Eihei Dōgen

1200–1253

Waka on Impermanence

The world? Moonlit
Drops shaken
From the crane's bill.

Translated from the Japanese by Lucien Stryk and Takashi Ikemoto.

Yosa Buson

1716–1784

The old man
cutting barley—
    bent like a sickle.

Translated from the Japanese by Robert Hass.

Lucia Perillo

1958–2016

I Could Name Some Names

of those who have drifted through thus far of
    their allotted
fifty or seventy or ninety years on Earth
with no disasters happening,
whatever had to be given up was given up—
the food at the rehab facility was better than you
    would expect
and the children turned out more or less okay;
sure there were some shaky years
but no one's living in the basement anymore
with a divot in his head where the shrapnel landed/or
don't look at her stump. It is easy
to feel possessed of a soul that's better schooled
than the fluffy cloud inside of people who have
    never known suchlike
events by which our darlings
are unfavorably remade. And the self
is the darling's darling
($I=darling^2$). Every day
I meditate against my envy

directed against those who drift inside the bubble
     of no-trouble
—what is the percentage? 20% of us? 8%? zero?
Maybe the ex-president with his nubile daughters,
vigorous old parents and clean colonoscopy. Grrrr.
Remember to breathe. *Breathe in suffering,*
and breathe out blessings say the ancient
     dharma texts.
Still I beg to file this one complaint:
that some are mountain-biking through
     the scrublands,
while she is here at Ralph's Thriftway,
running her thumb over a peach's bruise,
her leg a steel rod
in a mini-skirt, to make sure I see.

Han Shan

Ninth century

They laugh at me, "Hey farm boy!
Skinny head, your hat's not tall enough
and your belt goes around you twice!"
It's not that I don't know what's in . . .
If you don't have the cash, forget it.
But someday I'll get rich for sure,
and then I'll wear a big, tall
Buddhist gravestone on my head.

Translated from the Chinese by J. P. Seaton.

Jack Kerouac

1922–1969

In my medicine cabinet,
    the winter fly
has died of old age.

Ron Padgett

1942–

The Joke

When Jesus found himself
nailed to the cross,
crushed with despair,
crying out
"Why hast thou forsaken me?"
he enacted the story
of every person who suddenly realizes
not that he or she has been forsaken
but that there never was
a forsaker,
for the idea of immortality
that is the birthright of every human being
gradually vanishes
until it is gone
and we cry out.

PART TWO

Mindfulness

Billy Collins

1941–

Shoveling Snow with Buddha

In the usual iconography of the temple
    or the local Wok
you would never see him doing such a thing,
tossing the dry snow over a mountain
of his bare, round shoulder,
his hair tied in a knot,
a model of concentration.

Sitting is more his speed, if that is the word
for what he does, or does not do.

Even the season is wrong for him.
In all his manifestations, is it not warm or
    slightly humid?
Is this not implied by his serene expression,
that smile so wide it wraps itself around the waist of
    the universe?

But here we are, working our way down
    the driveway,
one shovelful at a time.

We toss the light powder into the clear air.
We feel the cold mist on our faces.
And with every heave we disappear
and become lost to each other
in these sudden clouds of our own making,
these fountain-bursts of snow.

This is so much better than a sermon in church,
I say out loud, but Buddha keeps on shoveling.
This is the true religion, the religion of snow,
and sunlight and winter geese barking in the sky,
I say, but he is too busy to hear me.

He has thrown himself into shoveling snow
as if it were the purpose of existence,
as if the sign of a perfect life were a clear driveway
you could back the car down easily
and drive off into the vanities of the world
with a broken heater fan and a song on the radio.

All morning long we work side by side,
me with my commentary
and he inside his generous pocket of silence,
until the hour is nearly noon
and the snow is piled high all around us;
then, I hear him speak.

After this, he asks,
can we go inside and play cards?

Certainly, I reply, and I will heat some milk
and bring cups of hot chocolate to the table
while you shuffle the deck,
and our boots stand dripping by the door.

Aaah, says the Buddha, lifting his eyes
and leaning for a moment on his shovel
before he drives the thin blade again
deep into the glittering white snow.

Wallace Stevens

1879–1955

The Snow Man

One must have a mind of winter
To regard the frost and the boughs
Of the pine-trees crusted with snow;

And have been cold a long time
To behold the junipers shagged with ice,
The spruces rough in the distant glitter

Of the January sun; and not to think
Of any misery in the sound of the wind,
In the sound of a few leaves,

Which is the sound of the land
Full of the same wind
That is blowing in the same bare place

For the listener, who listens in the snow,
And, nothing himself, beholds
Nothing that is not there and the nothing that is.

Kenneth Rexroth

1905–1982

Empty Mirror

As long as we are lost
In the world of purpose
We are not free. I sit
In my ten foot square hut.
The birds sing. The bees hum.
The leaves sway. The water
Murmurs over the rocks.
The canyon shuts me in.
If I moved, Bashō's frog
Would splash in the pool.
All summer long the gold
Laurel leaves fell through space.
Today I was aware
Of a maple leaf floating
On the pool. In the night
I stare into the fire.
Once I saw fire cities,
Towns, palaces, wars,
Heroic adventures,
In the campfires of youth.
Now I see only fire.

My breath moves quietly.
The stars move overhead.
In the clear darkness
Only a small red glow
Is left in the ashes.
On the table lies a cast
Snake skin and an uncut stone.

Gary Snyder

1930–

Piute Creek

One granite ridge
A tree, would be enough
Or even a rock, a small creek,
A bark shred in a pool.
Hill beyond hill, folded and twisted
Tough trees crammed
In thin stone fractures
A huge moon on it all, is too much.
The mind wanders. A million
Summers, night air still and the rocks
Warm. Sky over endless mountains.
All the junk that goes with being human
Drops away, hard rock wavers
Even the heavy present seems to fail
This bubble of a heart.
Words and books
Like a small creek off a high ledge
Gone in the dry air.

A clear, attentive mind
Has no meaning but that

Which sees is truly seen.
No one loves rock, yet we are here.
Night chills. A flick
In the moonlight
Slips into Juniper shadow:
Back there unseen
Cold proud eyes
Of Cougar or Coyote
Watch me rise and go.

Ikkyū Sojun

1394–1481

After ten years in the red-light district,
How solitary a spell in the mountains.
I can see clouds a thousand miles away,
Hear ancient music in the pines.

Translated from the Japanese by Lucien Stryk and Takashi Ikemoto.

William Stafford

1914–1993

Listening

My father could hear a little animal step,
or a moth in the dark against the screen,
and every far sound called the listening out
into places where the rest of us had never been.

More spoke to him from the soft wild night
than came to our porch for us on the wind;
we would watch him look up and his face go keen
till the walls of the world flared, widened.

My father heard so much that we still stand
inviting the quiet by turning the face,
waiting for a time when something in the night
will touch us too from that other place.

Dick Allen

1939–

Listening Deeply

Listening deeply,
sometimes—in another—you can hear
the sound of a hermit, sighing
as he climbs a mountain trail to reach
    a waterfall
or a Buddhist nun reciting prayers
while moonlight falls through the window
onto an old clay floor,
and once in a while, a child
rolling a hoop through the alleyways of Tokyo,
    laughing,
or a farmer pausing in a rice field to watch
    geese fly,
the thoughts on his lips he doesn't think to say.

D. H. Lawrence

1885–1930

The White Horse

The youth walks up to the white horse, to put
    its halter on
and the horse looks at him in silence.
They are so silent they are in another world.

A. R. Ammons

1926–2001

Clarifications

The crows, mingled
powder white,

arrive floundering
through the

heavy snowfall:
they land ruffling

stark black
on the spruce boughs and

chisel the neighborhood
sharp with their cries.

Denise Levertov

1923–1997

Aware

When I opened the door
I found the vine leaves
speaking among themselves in abundant
whispers.
       My presence made them
hush their green breath,
embarrassed, the way
humans stand up, buttoning their jackets,
acting as if they were leaving anyway, as if
the conversation had ended
just before you arrived.
            I liked
the glimpse I had, though,
of their obscure
gestures. I liked the sound
of such private voices. Next time
I'll move like cautious sunlight, open
the door by fractions, eavesdrop
peacefully.

Anna Swir

1909–1984

Our Two Silences

Silence
flows into me and out of me
washing my past away.
I am pure already, waiting for you. Bring me
your silence.

They will doze off
nestled in each other's arms,
our two silences.

Translated from the Polish by Czesław Miłosz and Leonard Nathan.

Wei Ying-Wu

737–792

In the Depths of West Mountain, Visiting the Master

A disciple for years at Twin-Stream,
what brings you to these mountains?

Great luminaries keep the world at war,
but your mind flowing-water idleness,

you swept tigers from forests, and now
sit alone, utter stillness. Guarding this

frontier, we double silence, wander
narrow passes where clouds are born.

Translated from the Chinese by David Hinton.

Yosa Buson

1716–1784

Coolness—
the sound of the bell
    as it leaves the bell.

Translated from the Japanese by Robert Hass.

Li Po

701–762

Watching a White Falcon Set Loose

High in September's frontier winds, white
brocade feathers, the Mongol falcon flies

alone, a flake of snow, a hundred miles
some fleeting speck of autumn in its eyes.

Translated from the Chinese by David Hinton.

William Carlos Williams

1883–1963

Fine Work with Pitch and Copper

Now they are resting
in the fleckless light
separately in unison

like the sacks
of sifted stone stacked
regularly by twos

about the flat roof
ready after lunch
to be opened and strewn

The copper in eight
foot strips has been
beaten lengthwise

down the center at right
angles and lies ready
to edge the coping

One still chewing
picks up a copper strip
and runs his eye along it.

Kobayashi Issa

1763–1828

The distant mountains
are reflected in the eye
of the Dragonfly

Translated from the Japanese by Sam Hamill.

A. R. Ammons
1926–2001

Reflective

I found a
weed
that had a

mirror in it
and that
mirror

looked in at
a mirror
in

me that
had a
weed in it

Adam Zagajewski

1945–

Auto Mirror

In the rear-view mirror suddenly
I saw the bulk of the Beauvais Cathedral;
great things dwell in small ones
for a moment.

Translated from the Polish by Clare Cavanagh and Benjamin Ivry.

Robert Frost

1874–1963

Tree at My Window

Tree at my window, window tree,
My sash is lowered when night comes on;
But let there never be curtain drawn
Between you and me.

Vague dreamhead lifted out of the ground
And thing next most diffuse to cloud,
Not all your light tongues talking aloud
Could be profound.

But tree, I have seen you taken and tossed,
And if you have seen me when I slept,
You have seen me when I was taken and swept
And all but lost.

That day she put our heads together,
Fate had her imagination about her,
Your head so much concerned with outer,
Mine with inner, weather.

Wisława Szymborska

1923–2012

No Title Required

It has come to this: I'm sitting under a tree
beside a river
on a sunny morning.
It's an insignificant event
and won't go down in history.
It's not battles and pacts,
where motives are scrutinized,
or noteworthy tyrannicides.

And yet I'm sitting by this river, that's a fact.
And since I'm here
I must have come from somewhere,
and before that
I must have turned up in many other places,
exactly like the conquerors of nations
before setting sail.

Even a passing moment has its fertile past,
its Friday before Saturday,
its May before June.

Its horizons are no less real
than those that a marshal's field glasses might scan.

This tree is a poplar that's been rooted here
        for years.
The river is the Raba; it didn't spring up yesterday.
The path leading through the bushes
wasn't beaten last week.
The wind had to blow the clouds here
before it could blow them away.

And though nothing much is going on nearby,
the world is no poorer in details for that.
It's just as grounded, just as definite
as when migrating races held it captive.

Conspiracies aren't the only things shrouded
        in silence.
Retinues of reasons don't trail coronations alone.
Anniversaries of revolutions may roll around,
but so do oval pebbles encircling the bay.

The tapestry of circumstance is intricate and dense.
Ants stitching in the grass.
The grass sewn into the ground.
The pattern of a wave being needled by a twig.

So it happens that I am and look.
Above me a white butterfly is fluttering
      through the air
on wings that are its alone,

and a shadow skims through my hands
that is none other than itself, no one else's
      but its own.

When I see such things, I'm no longer sure
that what's important
is more important than what's not.

Translated from the Polish by Stanisław Baranczak and Clare Cavanagh.

Bronisław Maj

1953–

A Leaf

A leaf, one of the last, parts from a maple branch:
it is spinning in the transparent air of October, falls
on a heap of others, stops, fades. No one
admired its entrancing struggle with the wind,
followed its flight, no one will distinguish it now
as it lies among other leaves, no one saw
what I did. I am
the only one.

Translated from the Polish by Czesław Miłosz and Robert Hass.

Ezra Pound

1885–1972

In a Station of the Metro

The apparition of these faces in the crowd;
petals on a wet, black bough.

Old Shōju

1642–1721

One look at plum blossoms
Opened Reiun's eyes,
Old Tan recites poems,
Is often in his cups.
Want "meaningless" Zen?
Just look—at anything!

Translated from the Japanese by Lucien Stryk and Takashi Ikemoto.

Ron Padgett
1942–

Now You See It

What you don't see
helps you see what
you do see: the keyhole
sharpens the thrill
in your brain,
even if there is
no one
in the room,
shadows
wafting across
the white sheets
as a song drifts in
the window,
her voice so pure
you can see
the face it rises from,
for what you see
helps you see what
you don't see.

Jane Hirshfield

1953–

Lighthouse

Its vision sweeps its one path
like an aged monk raking a garden,
his question long ago answered or moved on.
Far off, night-grazing horses,
breath scented with oatgrass and fennel,
step through it, disappear, step through it,
    disappear.

Ikkyū Sojun

1394–1481

Void in Form

When, just as they are,
White dewdrops gather
On scarlet maple leaves,
Regard the scarlet beads!

Translated from the Japanese by Lucien Stryk and Takashi Ikemoto.

Wallace Stevens

1879–1955

Study of Two Pears

I
Opusculum paedagogum.
The pears are not viols,
nudes or bottles.
They resemble nothing else.

II
They are yellow forms
Composed of curves
Bulging toward the base.
They are touched red.

III
They are not flat surfaces
Having curved outlines.
They are round
tapering toward the top.

IV

In the way they are modeled
There are bits of blue.
A hard dry leaf hangs
From the stem.

V

The yellow glistens.
It glistens with various yellows,
Citrons, oranges and greens
Flowering over the skin.

VI

The shadows of the pears
Are blobs on the green cloth.
The pears are not seen
As the observer wills.

Elizabeth Bishop

1911–1979

The Fish

I caught a tremendous fish
and held him beside the boat
half out of water, with my hook
fast in a corner of his mouth.
He didn't fight.
He hadn't fought at all.
He hung a grunting weight,
battered and venerable
and homely. Here and there
his brown skin hung in strips
like ancient wallpaper,
and its pattern of darker brown
was like wallpaper:
shapes like full-blown roses
stained and lost through age.
He was speckled with barnacles,
fine rosettes of lime,
and infested
with tiny white sea-lice,
and underneath two or three
rags of green weed hung down.

While his gills were breathing in
the terrible oxygen
—the frightening gills,
fresh and crisp with blood,
that can cut so badly—
I thought of the coarse white flesh
packed in like feathers,
the big bones and the little bones,
the dramatic reds and blacks
of his shiny entrails,
and the pink swim-bladder
like a big peony.
I looked into his eyes
which were far larger than mine
but shallower, and yellowed,
the irises backed and packed
with tarnished tinfoil
seen through the lenses
of old scratched isinglass.
They shifted a little, but not
to return my stare.
—It was more like the tipping
of an object toward the light.
I admired his sullen face,
the mechanism of his jaw,

and then I saw
that from his lower lip
—if you could call it a lip—
grim, wet, and weaponlike,
hung five old pieces of fish-line,
or four and a wire leader
with the swivel still attached,
with all their five big hooks
grown firmly in his mouth.
A green line, frayed at the end
where he broke it, two heavier lines,
and a fine black thread
still crimped from the strain and snap
when it broke and he got away.
Like medals with their ribbons
frayed and wavering,
a five-haired beard of wisdom
trailing from his aching jaw.
I stared and stared
and victory filled up
the little rented boat,
from the pool of bilge
where oil had spread a rainbow
around the rusted engine
to the bailer rusted orange,

the sun-cracked thwarts,
the oarlocks on their strings,
the gunnels—until everything
was rainbow, rainbow, rainbow!
And I let the fish go.

Robert Frost

1874–1963

Hyla Brook

By June our brook's run out of song and speed.
Sought for much after that, it will be found
Either to have gone groping underground
(And taken with it all the Hyla breed
That shouted in the mist a month ago,
Like ghost of sleigh-bells in a ghost of snow)—
Or flourished and come up in jewel-weed,
Weak foliage that is blown upon and bent
Even against the way its waters went.
Its bed is left a faded paper sheet
Of dead leaves stuck together by the heat—
A brook to none but who remember long.
This as it will be seen is other far
Than with brooks taken otherwhere in song.
We love the things we love for what they are.

Shido Bunan

1602–1676

The moon's the same old moon,
The flowers exactly as they were,
Yet I've become the thingness
Of all the things I see!

Translated from the Japanese by Lucien Stryk and Takashi Ikemoto.

Li Po

701–762

Zazen on Ching-t'ing Mountain

The birds have vanished down the sky.
Now the last cloud drains away.

We sit together, the mountain and me,
until only the mountain remains.

Translated from the Chinese by Sam Hamill.

Anna Swir

1909–1984

A Double Rapture

Because there is no me
and because I feel
how much there is no me.

Translated from the Polish by Czesław Miłosz and Leonard Nathan.

Gary Snyder
1930–

Mid-August at Sourdough Mountain Lookout

Down valley a smoke haze
Three days heat, after five days rain
Pitch glows on the fir-cones
Across rocks and meadows
Swarms of new flies.

I cannot remember things I once read
A few friends, but they are in cities.
Drinking cold snow-water from a tin cup
Looking down for miles
Through high still air.

Eihei Dōgen

1200–1253

This slowly drifting cloud is pitiful;
What dreamwalkers men become.
Awakened, I hear the one true thing—
Black rain on the roof of Fukakusa Temple.

Translated from the Japanese by Lucien Stryk and Takashi Ikemoto.

Ryōkan

1758–1831

The night is fresh and cool,
Staff in hand I walk through the gate.
Wisteria and ivy grow together along the winding
    mountain path;
Birds sing quietly in their nests and a monkey howls
    nearby.
As I reach a high peak a village appears in the
    distance.
The old pines are full of poems;
I bend down for a drink of pure spring water.
There is a gentle breeze, and the round moon hangs
    overhead.
Standing by a deserted building,
I pretend to be a crane softly floating among the
    clouds.

Translated from the Japanese by John Stevens.

Walt Whitman
1819–1892

I Stand and Look

I stand and look in the dark under a cloud,
But I see in the distance where the sun shines,
I see the thin haze on the tall white steeples
    of the city,—
I see the glistening of the waters in the distance.

Philip Larkin

1922–1985

Here

Swerving east, from rich industrial shadows
And traffic all night north; swerving through fields
Too thin and thistled to be called meadows,
And now and then a harsh-named halt, that shields
Workmen at dawn; swerving to solitude
Of skies and scarecrows, haystacks, hares
    and pheasants,
And the widening river's slow presence,
The piled gold clouds, the shining gull-marked mud,

Gathers to the surprise of a large town:
Here domes and statues, spires and cranes cluster
Beside grain-scattered streets, barge-crowded water,
And residents from raw estates, brought down
The dead straight miles by stealing flat-faced
    trolleys,
Push through plate-glass swing doors to
    their desires—
Cheap suits, red kitchen-ware, sharp shoes,
    iced lollies,
Electric mixers, toasters, washers, driers—

A cut-price crowd, urban yet simple, dwelling
Where only salesmen and relations come
Within a terminate and fishy-smelling
Pastoral of ships up streets, the slave museum,
Tattoo-shops, consulates, grim head-scarfed wives;
And out beyond its mortgaged half-built edges
Fast-shadowed wheat-fields, running high
    as hedges,
Isolate villages, where removed lives

Loneliness clarifies. Here silence stands
Like heat. Here leaves unnoticed thicken,
Hidden weeds flower, neglected waters quicken,
Luminously-peopled air ascends;
And past the poppies bluish neutral distance
Ends the land suddenly beyond a beach
Of shapes and shingle. Here is unfenced existence:
Facing the sun, untalkative, out of reach.

Elizabeth Bishop
1911–1979

Filling Station

Oh, but it is dirty!
—this little filling station,
oil-soaked, oil-permeated
to a disturbing, over-all
black translucency.
Be careful with that match!

Father wears a dirty,
oil-soaked monkey suit
that cuts him under the arms,
and several quick and saucy
and greasy sons assist him
(it's a family filling station),
all quite thoroughly dirty.

Do they live in the station?
It has a cement porch
behind the pumps, and on it
a set of crushed and grease-
impregnated wickerwork;
on the wicker sofa
a dirty dog, quite comfy.

Some comic books provide
the only note of color—
of certain color. They lie
upon a big dim doily
draping a taboret
(part of the set), beside
a big hirsute begonia.

Why the extraneous plant?
Why the taboret?
Why, oh why, the doily?
(Embroidered in daisy stitch
with marguerites, I think,
and heavy with gray crochet.)

Somebody embroidered the doily.
Somebody waters the plant,
or oils it, maybe. Somebody
arranges the rows of cans
so that they softly say:
Esso—so—so—so
to high-strung automobiles.
Somebody loves us all.

William Carlos Williams

1883–1963

The Poor

It's the anarchy of poverty
delights me, the old
yellow wooden house indented
among the new brick tenements

Or a cast-iron balcony
with panels showing oak branches
in full leaf. It fits
the dress of the children

reflecting every stage and
custom of necessity—
Chimneys, roofs, fences of
wood and metal in an unfenced

age and enclosing next to
nothing at all: the old man
in a sweater and soft black
hat who sweeps the sidewalk—

his own ten feet of it
in a wind that fitfully
turning his corner has
overwhelmed the entire city.

Kobayashi Issa

1763–1828

I'm going to roll over,
so please move,
      cricket.

Translated from the Japanese by Robert Hass.

Wisława Szymborska

1923–2012

Miracle Fair

The commonplace miracle:
that so many common miracles take place.

The usual miracles:
invisible dogs barking
in the dead of night.

One of many miracles:
a small and airy cloud
is able to upstage the massive moon.

Several miracles in one:
an alder is reflected in the water
and is reversed from left to right
and grows from crown to root
and never hits bottom
though the water isn't deep.

A run-of-the-mill miracle:
winds mild to moderate
turning gusty in storms.

A miracle in the first place:
cows will be cows.

Next but not least:
just this cherry orchard
from just this cherry pit.

A miracle minus top hat and tails:
fluttering white doves.

A miracle (what else can you call it):
the sun rose today at three fourteen A.M.
and will set tonight at one past eight.

A miracle that's lost on us:
the hand actually has fewer than six fingers
but still it's got more than four.

A miracle, just take a look around:
the inescapable earth.

An extra miracle, extra and ordinary:
the unthinkable
can be thought.

Translated from the Polish by Stanisław Barańczak and Clare Cavanagh.

Po Chü-i

772–846

Li the Mountain Recluse Stays the Night on Our Boat

It's dusk, my boat such tranquil silence,
mist rising over waters deep and still,

and to welcome a guest for the night,
there's evening wine, an autumn *ch'in*.

A master at the gate of Way, my visitor
arrives from exalted mountain peaks,

lofty cloudswept face raised all delight,
heart all sage clarity spacious and free.

Our thoughts begin where words end.
Refining dark-enigma depths, we gaze

quiet mystery into each other and smile,
sharing the mind that's forgotten mind.

Translated from the Chinese by David Hinton.

Matsuo Bashō

1644–1694

Wrapping the rice cakes
with one hand
    she fingers back her hair.

Translated from the Japanese by Robert Hass.

PART THREE

Joy

Ryōkan

1758–1831

First Days of Spring—the Sky

First days of Spring—the sky
is bright blue, the sun huge and warm.
Everything's turning green.
Carrying my monk's bowl, I walk to the village
to beg for my daily meal.
The children spot me at the temple gate
and happily crowd around,
dragging on my arms till I stop.
I put my bowl on a white rock,
hang my bag on a branch.
First we braid grasses and play tug-of-war,
then we take turns singing and keeping a kick-ball
    in the air:
I kick the ball and they sing, they kick and I sing.
Time is forgotten, the hours fly.
People passing by point at me and laugh:
"Why are you acting like such a fool?"
I nod my head and don't answer.

I could say something, but why?
Do you want to know what's in my heart?
From the beginning of time: just this! just this!

Translated from the Japanese by Stephen Mitchell.

Su Tung-P'o

1037–1101

With Mao and Fang, Visiting Bright Insight Monastery

It's enough on this twisting mountain road
    to simply stop.
Clear water cascades thin down rock, startling
    admiration,

white cloud swells of itself across ridgelines
    east and west,
and who knows if the lake's bright moon is above
    or below?

It's the season black and yellow millet both begin
    to ripen,
oranges red and green, halfway into such lovely
    sweetness.

All this joy in our lives—what is it but heaven's
    great gift?
Why confuse the children with all our fine
    explanations?

Translated from the Chinese by David Hinton.

Kobayashi Issa

1763–1828

Children imitating cormorants
are even more wonderful
than cormorants.

Translated from the Japanese by Robert Hass.

Ryōkan

1758–1831

Nothing satisfies some appetites,
but wild plants ease my hunger.

Free of untoward desires,
all things bring me pleasure.

Tattered robes warm frozen bones.
I wander with deer for companions.

I sing to myself like a crazy man
and children sing along.

Translated from the Japanese by Sam Hamill.

Chuang-Tzu

369–286 BCE

The Joy of Fishes

Chuang Tzu and Hui Tzu
Were crossing Hao river
By the dam.

Chuang said:
"See how free
The fishes leap and dart:
That is their happiness."

Hui replied:
"Since you are not a fish
How do you know
What makes fishes happy?"

Chuang said:
"Since you are not I
How can you possibly know
That I do not know
What makes fishes happy?"

Hui argued:
"If I, not being you,
Cannot know what you know
It follows that you
Not being a fish
Cannot know what they know."

Chuang said:
"Wait a minute!
Let us get back
To the original question.
What you asked me was
'How do you know
What makes fishes happy?'
From the terms of your question
You evidently know I know
What makes fishes happy.

"I know the joy of fishes
In the river
Through my own joy, as I go walking
Along the same river."

Translated from the Chinese by Thomas Merton.

Han Shan

Ninth century

The cloud road's choked with deep mist. No one
    gets here that way,
but these Heaven-Terrace Mountains have always
    been my home:

a place to vanish among five-thousand-foot cliffs
    and pinnacles,
ten thousand creeks and gorges all boulder towers
    and terraces.

I follow streams in birch-bark cap, wooden sandals,
    tattered robes,
and clutching a goosefoot walking-stick, circle back
    around peaks.

Once you realize this floating life is the perfect
    mirage of change,
it's breathtaking—this wild joy at wandering
    boundless and free.

Translated from the Chinese by David Hinton.

Matsuo Bashō

1644–1694

A field of cotton—
as if the moon
had flowered.

Translated from the Japanese by Lucien Stryk and Takashi Ikemoto.

Yosa Buson

1716–1784

Such a moon—
the thief
pauses to sing.

Translated from the Japanese by Lucien Stryk and Takashi Ikemoto.

Kobayashi Issa

1763–1828

Full moon;
my ramshackle hut
is what it is.

Translated from the Japanese by Robert Hass.

Matsuo Bashō

1644–1694

A cicada shell;
it sang itself
utterly away.

Translated from the Japanese by Robert Hass.

James Wright

1927–1980

A Blessing

Just off the highway to Rochester, Minnesota,
Twilight bounds softly forth on the grass.
And the eyes of those two Indian ponies
Darken with kindness.
They have come gladly out of the willows
To welcome my friend and me.
We step over the barbed wire into the pasture
Where they have been grazing all day, alone.
They ripple tensely, they can hardly contain
    their happiness
That we have come.
They bow shyly as wet swans. They love each other.
There is no loneliness like theirs.
At home once more, they begin munching
    the young tufts of spring in the darkness.
I would like to hold the slenderer one in my arms,
For she has walked over to me
And nuzzled my left hand.
She is black and white,
Her mane falls wild on her forehead,

And the light breeze moves me to caress
    her long ear
That is delicate as the skin over a girl's wrist.
Suddenly I realize
That if I stepped out of my body I would break
Into blossom.

Horses

From the window I saw the horses.
I was in Berlin, in winter. The light
was without light, the sky skyless.

The air white like a moistened loaf.

From my window, I could see a deserted arena,
a circle bitten out by the teeth of winter.

All at once, led out by a single man,
ten horses were stepping, stepping into the snow.

Scarcely had they rippled into existence
like flame, than they filled the whole world
    of my eyes,
empty till now. Faultless, flaming,
they stepped like ten gods on broad, clean hoofs,
their manes recalling a dream of salt spray.

Their rumps were globes, were oranges.

Their color was amber and honey, was on fire.

Their necks were towers
carved from the stone of pride,
and in their furious eyes, sheer energy
showed itself, a prisoner inside them.

And there, in the silence, at the mid-point
    of the day,
in a dirty, disgruntled winter,
the horses' intense presence was blood,
was rhythm, was the beckoning light of all being.

I saw, I saw, and seeing, I came to life.
There was the unwitting fountain, the dance of
    gold, the sky,
the fire that sprang to life in beautiful things.

I have obliterated that gloomy Berlin winter.

I shall not forget the light from those horses.

Translated from the Spanish by Alastair Reid.

Jack Gilbert
1925–2012

Horses at Midnight without a Moon

Our heart wanders lost in the dark woods.
Our dream wrestles in the castle of doubt.
But there's music in us. Hope is pushed down
but the angel flies up again taking us with her.
The summer mornings begin inch by inch
while we sleep, and walk with us later
as long-legged beauty through
the dirty streets. It is no surprise
that danger and suffering surround us.
What astonishes is the singing.
We know the horses are there in the dark
meadow because we can smell them,
can hear them breathing.
Our spirit persists like a man struggling
through the frozen valley
who suddenly smells flowers
and realizes the snow is melting
out of sight on top of the mountain,
knows that spring has begun.

Kobayashi Issa

1763–1828

Under cherry trees
there are
no strangers

Translated from the Japanese by Lucien Stryk and Takashi Ikemoto.

Tomas Tranströmer

1931–2015

Face to Face

In February living stood still.
The birds flew unwillingly and the soul
chafed against the landscape as a boat
chafes against the pier it lies moored to.

The trees stood with their backs turned to me.
The deep snow was measured with dead straws.
The footprints grew old out on the crust.
Under a tarpaulin language pined.

One day something came to the window.
Work was dropped. I looked up.
The colors flared. Everything turned around.
The earth and I sprang toward each other.

Translated from the Swedish by Robin Fulton.

Marilyn Krysl

1942–

She Speaks a Various Language

The floor is cold
the ground frozen
This is the bottom
All the world's seeds have wound down

And just when the stem of my spine
seems to have dried up
and become a stalk
on which my head merely nods

just when I think nothing is left alive

the bare branches of the trees
rise up, beckoning

And it isn't simply
that I want to go out to them
They also want me to come

Come, they say in their motion
in their scraping of branch against branch
like a woman rubbing her hands together

Come with us   where we are going
Walk with us   up into the wind

Saigyō
1118–1190

Quiet mountain hut
by a rice patch . . . till a deer's cry
just outside startles me
and I move . . . so startling him:
we astonish one another.

Translated from the Japanese by William LeFleur.

William Stafford

1914–1993

It's All Right

Someone you trusted has treated you bad.
Someone has used you to vent their ill temper.
Did you expect anything different?
Your work—better than some others'—has
    languished,
neglected. Or a job you tried was too hard,
and you failed. Maybe weather or bad luck
spoiled what you did. That grudge, held against you
for years after you patched up, has flared,
and you've lost a friend for a time. Things
at home aren't so good; on the job your spirits
have sunk. But just when the worst bears down
you find a pretty bubble in your soup at noon,
and outside at work a bird says, "Hi!"
Slowly the sun creeps along the floor;
it is coming your way. It touches your shoe.

Jacques Prévert

1900–1977

The Dunce

He says no with his head
but he says yes with his heart
he says yes to what he loves
he says no to the teacher
he stands
he is questioned
and all the problems are posed
sudden mad laughter seizes him
and he erases all
the words and figures
names and dates
sentences and snares
and despite the teacher's threats
to the jeers of infant prodigies
with chalk of every color
on the blackboard of misfortune
he draws the face of happiness.

Translated from the French by Lawrence Ferlinghetti.

Walt Whitman

1819–1892

When I Heard the Learn'd Astronomer

When I heard the learn'd astronomer,
When the proofs, the figures, were ranged
   in columns before me,
When I was shown the charts and diagrams,
   to add, divide, and measure them,
When I sitting heard the astronomer where he
   lectured with much applause in the
   lecture-room,
How soon unaccountable I became tired and sick,
Till rising and gliding out I wander'd off by myself,
In the mystical moist night-air, and from
   time to time,
Look'd up in perfect silence at the stars.

Yosa Buson

1716–1784

My arm for a pillow,
I really like myself
     under the hazy moon.

Translated from the Japanese by Robert Hass.

Po Chü-i

772–846

After *Quiet Joys at South Garden* Sent by P'ei Tu

This hut isolate and clear beside the pond:
surely this is what lofty thoughts must be,

blinds in the occasional breeze stirring,
a bridge shining late sun back into water.

I've grown quiet here, company to cranes,
and so idle I'm like any other cloud adrift.

Why bother to go study under Duke Liu
or search wild peaks for Master Red Pine?

Translated from the Chinese by David Hinton.

William Stafford

1914–1993

Ask Me

Some time when the river is ice ask me
mistakes I have made. Ask me whether
what I have done is my life. Others
have come in their slow way into
my thought, and some have tried to help
or to hurt: ask me what difference
their strongest love or hate has made.

I will listen to what you say.
You and I can turn and look
at the silent river and wait. We know
the current is there, hidden; and there
are comings and goings from miles away
that hold the stillness exactly before us.
What the river says, that is what I say.

Pablo Neruda

1904–1973

Ode to My Socks

Maru Mori brought me
a pair
of socks
knitted with her own
shepherd's hands,
two socks soft
as rabbits.
I slipped
my feet into them
as if
into
jewel cases
woven
with threads of
dusk
and sheep's wool

Audacious socks,
my feet became
two woolen
fish,

two long sharks
of lapis blue
shot
with a golden thread,
two mammoth blackbirds,
two cannons,
thus honored
were
my feet
by
these
celestial
socks.
They were
so beautiful
that for the first time
my feet seemed
unacceptable to me,
two tired old
fire fighters
not worthy
of the woven
fire
of those luminous
socks.

Nonetheless,
I resisted
the strong temptation
to save them
the way schoolboys
bottle
fireflies,
the way scholars
hoard
sacred documents.
I resisted
the wild impulse
to place them in a cage
of gold
and daily feed them
birdseed
and rosy melon flesh.
Like explorers who in the forest
surrender a rare
and tender deer
to the spit
and eat it
with remorse,
I stuck out my feet
and pulled on

the
handsome
socks,
and then my shoes.

So this is
the moral of my ode:
twice beautiful
is beauty
and what is good is doubly
good
when it is a case of two
woolen socks
in wintertime.

Translated from the Spanish by Margaret Sayers Peden.

Ron Padgett

1942–

Inaction of Shoes

There are many things to be done today
and it's a lovely day to do them in

Each thing a joy to do
and a joy to have done

I can tell because of the calm I feel
when I think about doing them

I can almost hear them say to me
Thank you for doing us

And when evening comes
I'll remove my shoes and place them on the floor

And think how good they look
sitting? . . . standing? . . . there

Not doing anything

Anna Swir

1909–1984

Priceless Gifts

An empty day without events.
And that is why
it grew immense
as space. And suddenly
happiness of being
entered me.

I heard
in my heartbeat
the birth of time
and each instant of life
one after the other
came rushing in
like priceless gifts.

Translated from the Polish by Czesław Miłosz and Leonard Nathan.

Yannis Ritsos
1909–1990

January 21

A cessation.
You're not searching.
How nice it is tonight.
Two birds fell asleep in your pockets.

*Translated from the Greek by Edmund Keeley and Karen
Emmerich.*

A. R. Ammons

1926–2002

Stills

I have nowhere
to go and

nowhere to go

when I get
back from there.

Han Shan

Ninth century

My old landlady
got rich a couple years ago.
Used to be poorer than me.
Now she laughs that I don't have money.
She laughs that I've fallen behind.
I laugh that she's gotten ahead.
Both of us laughing, no stopping us.
Lady of the Land, and the Lord of the West.

Translated from the Chinese by J. P. Seaton.

Fernando Pessoa

1888–1935

Calm because I'm unknown,
And myself because I'm calm,
I want to fill my days
With wanting nothing from them.

For those whom wealth touches,
Gold irritates the skin.
For those on whom fame blows,
Life fogs over.

On those for whom happiness
Is their sun, night will fall.
But those who hope for nothing
Are glad for whatever comes.

Translated from the Portuguese by Richard Zenith.

Tracy K. Smith

1972–

Credulity

We believe we are giving ourselves away,
And so it feels good,
Our bodies swimming together
In afternoon light, the music
That enters our window as far
From the voices that made it
As our own minds are from reason.
There are whole doctrines on loving.
A science. I would like to know everything
About convincing love to give me
What it does not possess to give. And then
I would like to know how to live with nothing.
Not memory. Nor the taste of the words
I have willed you whisper into my mouth.

Billy Collins

1941–

Aimless Love

This morning as I walked along the lakeshore,
I fell in love with a wren
and later in the day with a mouse
the cat had dropped under the dining room table.

In the shadows of an autumn evening,
I fell for a seamstress
still at her machine in the tailor's window,
and later for a bowl of broth,
steam rising like smoke from a naval battle.

This is the best kind of love, I thought,
without recompense, without gifts,
or unkind words, without suspicion,
or silence on the telephone.

The love of the chestnut,
the jazz cap and one hand on the wheel.

No lust, no slam of the door—
the love of the miniature orange tree,

the clean white shirt, the hot evening shower,
the highway that cuts across Florida.

No waiting, no huffiness, or rancor—
just a twinge every now and then

for the wren who had built her nest
on a low branch overhanging the water
and for the dead mouse,
still dressed in its light brown suit.

But my heart is always propped up
in a field on its tripod,
ready for the next arrow.

After I carried the mouse by the tail
to a pile of leaves in the woods,
I found myself standing at the bathroom sink
gazing down affectionately at the soap,
so patient and soluble,
so at home in its pale green soap dish
I could feel myself falling again
as I felt its turning in my wet hands
and caught the scent of lavender and stone.

Jack Gilbert

1925–2012

A Brief for the Defense

Sorrow everywhere. Slaughter everywhere. If babies
are not starving someplace, they are starving
somewhere else. With flies in their nostrils.
But we enjoy our lives because that's what
    God wants.

Otherwise the mornings before summer dawn
    would not
be made so fine. The Bengal tiger would not
be fashioned so miraculously well. The poor women
at the fountain are laughing together between
the suffering they have known and the awfulness
in their future, smiling and laughing while
    somebody
in the village is very sick. There is laughter
every day in the terrible streets of Calcutta,
and the women laugh in the cages of Bombay.
If we deny our happiness, resist our satisfaction,
we lessen the importance of their deprivation.
We must risk delight. We can do without pleasure,
but not delight. Not enjoyment. We must have

the stubbornness to accept our gladness in
    the ruthless
furnace of this world. To make injustice the only
measure of our attention is to praise the Devil.
If the locomotive of the Lord runs us down,
we should give thanks that the end had magnitude.
We must admit there will be music despite
    everything.
We stand at the prow again of a small ship
anchored late at night in the tiny port
looking over to the sleeping island: the waterfront
is three shuttered cafés and one naked light
    burning.
To hear the faint sound of oars in the silence
    as a rowboat
comes slowly out and then goes back is truly worth
all the years of sorrow that are to come.

A. R. Ammons

1926–2002

The City Limits

When you consider the radiance, that it does not
    withhold itself
but pours its abundance without selection into
    every nook
and cranny not overhung or hidden;
    when you consider

that birds' bones make no awful noise
    against the light
but lie low in the light as in a high testimony;
    when you consider
the radiance, that it will look into the guiltiest

swervings of the weaving heart and bear
    itself upon them,
not flinching into disguise or darkening;
    when you consider
the abundance of such resource as illuminates
    the glow-blue

bodies and gold-skeined wings of flies
    swarming the dumped
guts of a natural slaughter or the coil of shit
    and in no way
winces from its storms of generosity;
    when you consider

that air or vacuum, snow or shale, squid or wolf,
    rose or lichen,
each is accepted into as much light as it will take,
    then the heart
moves roomier, the man stands and looks
    about, the

leaf does not increase itself above the grass,
    and the dark
work of the deepest cells is of a tune
    with May bushes
and fear lit by the breadth of such calmly
    turns to praise.

Marianne Moore

1887–1972

What Are Years?

What is our innocence,
what is our guilt? All are
naked, none is safe. And whence
is courage: the unanswered question,
the resolute doubt,—
dumbly calling, deafly listening—that
in misfortune, even death,
encourages others
and in its defeat, stirs

the soul to be strong? He
sees deep and is glad, who
accedes to mortality
and in his imprisonment rises
upon himself as
the sea in a chasm, struggling to be
free and unable to be,
in its surrendering
finds its continuing.

So he who strongly feels,
behaves. The very bird,
grown taller as he sings, steels
his form straight up. Though he is captive,
his mighty singing
says, satisfaction is a lowly
thing, how pure a thing is joy.
This is mortality,
this is eternity.

Alicia Ostriker

1937–

Wrinkly Lady Dancer

Going to be an old wrinkly lady
Going to be one of those frail rag people
Going to have withered hands and be
Puzzled to tears crossing the street

Hobble cautiously onto buses
Like a withery fruit
And quite silently sitting in this lurching bus
The avenues coming by

Some other passengers gaze at me
Clutching my cane and my newspaper
Seemingly protectively, but I will really be
    thinking about
The afternoon I danced naked with you
The afternoon I danced naked with you
The afternoon! I danced! Naked with you!

William Carlos Williams

1883–1963

To Waken an Old Lady

Old age is
a flight of small
cheeping birds
skimming
bare trees
above a snow glaze.
Gaining and failing
they are buffeted
by a dark wind—
But what?
On harsh weedstalks
the flock has rested—
the snow
is covered with broken
seed husks
and the wind tempered
by a shrill
piping of plenty.

Jack Gilbert

1925–2012

Getting Old

The soft wind comes sweet in the night
on the mountain. Invisible except for
the sound it makes in the big poplars outside
and the feel on his naked, single body,
which breathes quietly a little before dawn,
eyes open and in love with the table
and chair in the transparent dark and stars
in the other window. Soon it will be time
for the first tea and cool pear and then
the miles down and miles up the mountain.
"Old and alone," he thinks, smiling.
Full of what abundance has done to his spirit.
Feeling around inside to see if his heart
is still, thank God, ambitious. The way
old men look in their eyes each morning.
Knowing she isn't there and how much Michiko
isn't anywhere. The eyes close as he remembers
seeing the big owl on the roof last night
for the first time after hearing it for months.
Thinking how much he has grown unsuited

for love the size it is for him. "But maybe not," he says. And the eyes open as he grins at the heart's stubborn pretending.

Ron Padgett

1942–

Words from the Front

We don't look as young
as we used to
except in the dim light
especially in
the soft warmth of candlelight
when we say
in all sincerity
You're so cute
and
You're my cutie.
Imagine
two old people
behaving like this.
It's enough
to make you happy.

Paulann Petersen

1942–

Why the Aging Poet Continues to Write

At a coneflower's seed-making center,
hundreds of tiny dark florets—
each stiff and sharp—
take turns oozing
their flashes of pollen.
A flagrant
bee-stopping show.

Making a bright circle,
the outermost spiky blossoms
open first to then fade.
Shrinking day by day,
the ring of yellow flame
moves inward.
That heart—what's at
the flower's very core—
blazes last.

A. R. Ammons

1926–2002

Old Geezer

The quickest
way
to change

the
world is
to

like it
the
way it

is.

Ryōkan

1758–1831

Don't say my hut has nothing to offer:
come and I will share with you
the cool breeze that fills my window.

Translated from the Japanese by John Stevens.

Appendices

Mindful Reading

Mindfulness enhances everything we do: walking in the woods, washing the dishes, listening to music, looking at a tree, even taking out the garbage. As with all these experiences, the more mindful we are when we read poems—the more we can cultivate an open, receptive, nonjudging awareness in our reading—the richer our experience will be. How can we learn to bring the same quality of attention to poetry that we bring to meditation practice?

When we sit in meditation, we shift from *thinking about* our life to *experiencing* whatever arises in the present moment: bodily sensations, sounds, feelings, the breath. Thoughts will happen, too, but we learn not to indulge or chase after them. We simply notice them as one more strand in the intricate texture of the present moment.

But what happens when we read a poem? Here the analytical mind wants to take charge, wants to turn the poem into a problem to be solved, a code to be cracked, a secret to be revealed. For whatever reason—trauma suffered in high school English class, intimidation before a sometimes strange and difficult art, the anxiety of not getting it right—we too often bypass the pleasures of experiencing the poem and go straight to the work of interpreting it, hoping to figure out "what it means." But this relentless need to know, to understand, is often just another manifestation of the ego's need to control, to reduce slippery reality to manageable thought. John Keats described being free of this need to know as a "Negative Capability . . . when a man is capable of being in uncertainties, mysteries, doubts, without any irritable reaching after fact and reason." He went on to say that "with a great poet, the sense of Beauty overcomes every other consideration, or rather obliterates all consideration."

If we allow ourselves to be at ease with uncertainty and mystery, and if we can savor what's beautiful and pleasurable about a poem, our experience will be quite different, and much richer, than if we just *think* about what a poem is saying. And it's here that mindfulness practice can help.

Just as we shift from thinking to experiencing in meditation, when we read a poem we can also focus on noticing and appreciating rather than interpreting and explaining. We can immerse ourselves in the poem's atmosphere, its tones and textures, its sounds and images and rhythms, the way it moves and how it feels, the details of how it's made. Doing so requires no special literary training. What's needed mainly is alertness and curiosity, a willingness to *be with* what is happening in the poem without worrying too much about what it means. Poems do communicate ideas, but they are much more than a mechanism for communicating ideas. We don't read a poem the way we read a set of instructions or a newspaper or a philosophical argument. We look *at* the language as well as through it; we relish it, experience it sensually as well as conceptually. And the longer we can stay with the poem on the level of noticing and sensing rather than thinking and explaining, the more we will enjoy it. In his mock manifesto, "Personism," Frank O'Hara downgrades the importance of ideas in poems: "I'm not saying that I don't have practically the most lofty ideas of anyone writing today, but what difference does that make? They're just ideas. The only good thing about it is that when I get lofty enough I've stopped thinking and that's when refreshment arrives."

In "Introduction to Poetry," Billy Collins describes trying to get his students to enjoy rather than interrogate a poem. He wants his students to "walk inside the poem's room / and feel the walls for a light switch" or to "waterski across the surface of a poem / waving at the author's name on the shore."

> *But all they want to do*
> *is tie the poem to a chair with rope*
> *and torture a confession out of it.*

> *They begin beating it with a hose*
> *to find out what it really means.*

So, how do we enter a poem with openness, gentleness, and a lively curiosity rather than an irritable need to know? As in meditation, the first step is to simply notice what's happening, to see *how* the poem is saying what it's saying. Is the voice of the poem serious or humorous, intense or relaxed, formal or informal? Are the lines long or short, rhymed or unrhymed, smooth or jagged? Does the poem move quickly, like O'Hara's "The Day Lady Died," or slowly, like Tu Fu's "Jade Flower Palace"? Is the poem immersed in the physical world, as in Philip Larkin's "Here," or is it a poem of abstract statements, like Fernando Pessoa's "Calm because I'm unknown"? Is it a single gesture, a single striking image, like A. R. Ammons's "Clarifications," or a series of careful observations, as in Ruth Stone's "Train Ride" or Elizabeth Bishop's "The Fish"? Does the poem feel playful and affectionate, like Ron Padgett's "Words from the Front," or heartbreaking, like Kobayashi Issa's "Mother I never knew" or Andrea Hollander's "October 9, 1970"? Poems have many ways of being in the world, an almost infinite variety; they ask us to notice their unique way of doing what they do.

Most important is to notice what you enjoy about a poem and let yourself savor it. A poem must first of all give pleasure. No one will stay with a poem for long if it doesn't give pleasure, no matter how significant its subject. But poems are not obliged to make perfect sense, and sometimes they don't, or not right away. As Wallace Stevens said, "The poem must resist the intelligence almost successfully." If you encounter something in a poem that isn't immediately clear, the mind will want to engage that, like a terrier with a rag doll. But don't worry about it. Let the line or passage rest in the soft light of incomprehension, along with all the other things you don't know or fully understand. The Chinese Zen master Dizang said, "Not knowing is most intimate." But when you read lines that seem especially lit up—that move or intrigue you in some way, or that are simply pleasing or even dazzling—don't focus on what they might mean, or on being able to formulate a statement about what they might mean, as if you

might be called upon to explain the poem, to your-
self or to someone else. No one will quiz you! Just
linger with those poems or passages that resonate
with you: notice how you feel when you read them,
the emotional weather they cast over you, the way
they sound and move. Let them live inside you for
a while; rest your mind on them the way you might
rest it on the breath. The longer you can just sit with
the poem, the more it will reveal. But it doesn't really
require effort—just presence, alertness, patience,
care. Mindfulness, in other words.

Meditation on Sounds

One practice that can deepen mindful reading of poetry is meditating on sounds. Because sound is such a vital aspect of poetry, meditation that heightens our awareness of sound can help us hear poems with greater openness and sensitivity. A number of poems in the anthology are explicitly about sound, listening, or silence: William Stafford's "Listening," Dick Allen's "Listening Deeply," Denise Levertov's "Aware," D. H. Lawrence's "The White Horse," Anna Swir's "Our Two Silences," Wei Ying-Wu's "In the Depths of West Mountain, Visiting the Master" and Yosa Buson's "Coolness." You may want to read these poems before you begin this meditation, though it is not necessary. If you do read them, just experience them without thinking too much about them.

Choose a length of time for your mediation, set a timer, and place the anthology within easy reach. Once you have settled into your meditation posture, bring your attention to the breath. Simply notice the physical sensations of breathing: the rise and fall of the abdomen, air flowing in and out of the nostrils. Be aware also of whatever body sensations are present: a tingling in the feet, an ache in the low back, a tightness in the jaw, your contact with the cushion or chair. Just notice what's happening in the body without judging, without trying to push away unpleasant sensations or to prolong pleasant ones.

Now let your awareness expand to include the sounds occurring inside and outside the room. Cultivate a wide open acceptance of whatever sounds appear: cars passing, crows cawing, appliances humming, a neighbor's lawn mower, sirens in the distance, birdsong, the gurgling of your own stomach. These ambient sounds are sometimes referred to as "the Buddha's orchestra," the music of life.

As you sit in meditation, don't go looking for sounds; just receive without judgment whatever sounds arise. If an unpleasant sound appears, don't regard it as a disruption or an impediment to your concentration. Turn your attention to it and embrace it with interest and curiosity. Don't get caught up in identifying or creating a story about the sounds you hear. Instead, notice their impermanent nature, the way they arise, last for a while, and then vanish back into silence. You'll find that when you listen closely in this way, even sounds that seem more or less constant are changing in subtle ways. See if you can stay with a sound for its entire lifespan: from its appearance, through its changes, to its disappearance. After a while, your sense of a separate listener "in here" and sounds "out there" may fall away: hearing is just happening. If your attention wanders during the meditation, as it surely will, simply acknowledge that by noting "wandering" and return to a spacious awareness of sound.

When you reach the end of the meditation, open the anthology at random and read aloud the first poem you find. Bring the same attention to the poem that you've just been bringing to sounds. Close your eyes and see if you can enter the poem without thinking about it. Let yourself feel and hear and visualize it. Allow yourself to inhabit the space the poem creates: a little room opened by the words, or a boundless emptiness. Notice whatever feelings the poem elicits in you, whatever physical sensations and emotions arise in the meditative field of awareness. Read the poem again, this time silently, but attend to sound and rhythm especially. Feel into the mood of the poem, which is intimately connected to its sound, and let that mood color your own inner state like a drop of ink falling into a calm, clear pond. Don't worry about what the poem might mean, or how to frame your reaction to it in words. Just sit with it in the light of awareness for a few minutes, or as long as the poem resonates with you. Listen to it, savor it, carry it with you throughout the day.

Biographical Notes

Dick Allen (1939–) grew up near the Adirondack Mountains in Round Lake, New York. He served as Connecticut's poet laureate from 2010 to 2015 and is the author of numerous poetry collections, including *The Zen Master Poems, Present Vanishing,* and *Ode to the Cold War: Poems New and Selected.* His work has been included in several Best American Poetry and Best American Spiritual Writing anthologies. Of his process, Allen has observed, "I like how poetry can 'leap' so suddenly from here to there—like the mind's sudden leaps. I like how the unexpected can fly into a poem and out, the real and the mystical, the personal and the universal can merge."

A. R. Ammons (1926–2001) was born in rural North Carolina, near Whiteville, and grew up on a cotton and tobacco farm during the Great Depression. Like James Schuyler and Frank O'Hara, Ammons served on an escort destroyer as a sonar man, or "ping jockey," during World

War II. After the war, he studied biology at Wake Forest University and literature at the University of California, Berkeley. He was vice president of a biological glass factory in New Jersey before joining the faculty at Cornell University, where he taught for many years. Ammons twice won the National Book Award—for his *Collected Poems* in 1973 and for *Garbage* in 1993, a book-length poem about the transfiguration of matter into spirit, spirit into matter, "stone into wind, wind into stone." Ammons extended the Emersonian tradition, which he recast through a scientific understanding of natural processes, but was also strongly influenced by Taoist thought. In his most famous poem, "Corson's Inlet," Ammons enacts "the overall wandering of mirroring mind," a stance toward natural processes that ultimately derives from ancient Chinese poets. Echoing Lao Tzu, Ammons said that poetry is "a verbal means to a non-verbal source . . . a motion to no-motion, to the still point of contemplation and deep realization. Its knowledges are all negative and, therefore, more positive than any knowledge. Nothing that can be said about it in words is worth saying."

Matsuo Bashō (1644–1694) was born in Ueno, thirty miles southwest of Kyoto, and became the most famous poet of the Edo period, a master of both haiku and *renga* (linked haiku). Bashō, more than any other poet, lifted haiku from a literary pastime into a major poetic form. He studied poetry and Zen in Kyoto as a young man and later became a Buddhist monk. His early poetry followed the conventions of the day and was received with great admiration. He became a *haikaishi,* or professional teacher of poetry, taking students and correcting verses for a fee. But in 1678, following the example of Po Chü-i, Bashō distanced himself from literary life and retired to a simple gamekeeper's hut. He was deeply influenced by Chinese literature, particularly the T'ang poets Li Po, Tu Fu, and Han Shan, as well as Po Chü-i. The twelfth-century Japanese wandering poet-monk Saigyō was also a major influence, particularly on Bashō's own masterpiece of poetic journeying, *Narrow Road to the Deep North.* Though strongly influenced by ancient poets, Bashō was also radically innovative. "Do not seek to follow in the footsteps of the wise," he wrote, "seek what they sought." Bashō's later poetry is colored by *wabi-sabi,* an aesthetic that evokes loneliness, melancholy, impermanence, and intimacy and favors simplicity, naturalness, modesty, and imperfection. After years of wandering, he returned to Edo in 1691 but became disillusioned with literary life in the capital and retired once again to a *bashō* (banana tree leaf) hut provided by his disciples and from which he had taken his name. He fell ill during a trip to Osaka and died there in 1694.

Ellen Bass (1947–) grew up in Ventor, New Jersey. She studied with Anne Sexton at Boston University, and she credits Sexton with rescuing her from the critical discouragement she received from other teachers there. In addition to her books of poetry—including *The Human Line* and *Like a Beggar*—Bass coedited with Florence Howe the groundbreaking anthology of feminist poetry, *No More Masks!* She has also coauthored with Laura Davis *The Courage to Heal: A Guide for Women Survivors of Child Sexual Abuse,* and with Kate Kaufman, *Free Your Mind: The Book for Gay, Lesbian and Bisexual Youth.* The influence of Buddhist thought is clear in Bass's poetry. Responding to the question of feeling exposed in her poems, Bass said in an interview that it's not in her choice of subjects that she feels exposed but in revealing how her mind works. "That's where I think the risk is. And maybe that's why people often feel so scared when they share their poetry—because you're exposing what it's like to be in your mind. That's intimate. I think that's the intimacy of poetry." Bass lives in Santa Cruz, California, and teaches in the low-residency MFA program at Pacific University.

Elizabeth Bishop (1911–1979) was born in Worcester, Massachusetts, but spent much of her childhood in Great Village, Nova Scotia. Her father died when she was eight months old, and her mother, who had suffered serious mental illness for many years, had to be permanently institutionalized when Bishop was just five, a traumatic experience Bishop wrote about in her short story "The Village." She attended Vassar, where she met Marianne Moore, whose friendship strongly influenced the young poet's early writing, just as Robert Lowell would influence her later work. Bishop lived in Boston, Key West, and New York, but spent much of her adult life in Brazil with her partner, the architect Lota de Macedo Soares, who later committed suicide in New York City. Bishop herself struggled with depression and alcoholism for many years. She prized accuracy of observation in her poetry (she was also a fine watercolorist), and her poems exhibit a remarkable degree of mindfulness. In a letter to her biographer,

Anne Stevenson, she said, "What one seems to want in art, in experiencing it, is the same thing that is necessary for its creation, a self-forgetful, perfectly useless concentration." She won the Pulitzer Prize in 1956 and the National Book Award in 1970.

Shido Bunan (1602–1676) was a Japanese Zen master in the Tokogawa period. Bunan lived an austere life as a lay innkeeper, practicing Zen under the guidance of the Rinzai teacher Gudō Toshoku and producing much poetry and prose. His own most famous student, Shōju-rojin, would become the root teacher of Hakuin Ekaku Zenji. Thomas Cleary has translated Bunan's sayings in *The Original Face*.

Yosa Buson (1716–1784) was born twenty-two years after the death of Matsuo Bashō in Kema, a suburb of Osaka just thirty miles from Kyoto. With Bashō and Kobayashi Issa, he is considered among the greatest haiku poets. He was also a master painter and during his own life was more renowned for his painting than his poetry. Little is known about his early life, but both his parents died when he was quite young. He moved to Edo when he was twenty and studied haiku with Hayano Hahjin, a disciple of Bashō, and attended lectures on T'ang poetry and the Confucian classics. When he was twenty-six he left Edo and spent the next ten years wandering the northern provinces painting and writing poetry. He retraced Bashō's journeys and produced illustrated versions of *Narrow Road to the Deep North.* Like Bashō, he practiced Pure Land Buddhism. In 1751 he settled in Kyoto, taking the place of his former poetry teacher and continuing to have success as a painter. When asked by a student if there was a secret to writing haiku, Buson replied, "Yes, use the commonplace to escape the commonplace." When the student asked how, he said, "Read Chinese poetry."

Chuang-Tzu (369–286 BCE) is the most important Taoist philosopher after Lao-Tzu. He wrote prose commentaries on the *Tao Te Ching,* as well as poems and parables. Little is known about his life, and some scholars doubt his existence—a doubt that Chuang-Tzu himself would perhaps have shared. A brief sketch of Chuang-Tzu appears in chapter 63 of Sima Qian's *Records of the Grand Historian:* "Chuang-Tzu had made himself well acquainted with all the literature of his time, but preferred the views of Lao-Tzu; and ranked himself among his followers, so that of the more than ten myriads of characters contained in his published writings the greater part are occupied with metaphorical illustrations of Lao's doctrines. . . . Chuang was an admirable writer and skillful composer, and by his instances and truthful descriptions hit and exposed the Mohists and Literati. The ablest scholars of his day could not escape his satire nor reply to it, while he allowed and enjoyed himself with his sparkling, dashing style; and thus it was that the greatest men, even kings and princes, could not use him for their purposes." Witty, mystical, delightfully playful, Chuang-Tzu argued for the practice of nondoing, of not interfering with the already perfect nature of things. "For the duck's legs, though short, cannot be lengthened without causing dismay to the duck."

Billy Collins (1941–) was born in Manhattan and grew up in Queens and White Plains, New York. He received a BA in English from the College of the Holy Cross in 1963 and both an MA and PhD in Romantic Poetry from the University of California, Riverside. Collins served two terms as the United States Poet Laureate, from 2001 to 2003, and was the New York State Poet Laureate from 2004 to 2006. He is a regular guest on National Public Radio programs, including Garrison Keillor's *Writer's Almanac*. His poems are notable for their humor, accessibility, and charm; his meditations on daily life, or on such subjects as history, art, and poetry itself, often take unexpected, whimsical turns. The critic John Taylor wrote of Collins: "Rarely has anyone written poems that appear so transparent on the surface yet become so ambiguous, thought-provoking, or simply wise once the reader has peered into the depths."

Eihei Dōgen (1200–1253), a highly influential figure in Zen Buddhism, was born in Kyoto into a noble family, though he was orphaned by age seven. He studied the Buddhist scriptures on Mount Hiei, the center of Tendai Buddhism, and was an ordained monk by the age of thirteen. He grew restless with the emphasis placed on koan study at the neglect of the sutras and in 1223 made the perilous voyage to China, where he spent four years in intensive study of Zen. He attained enlightenment under the master Ju-ching and returned to Japan in 1227, where he founded the Soto school of Zen. Highly regarded for both his poetry and his philosophical writings, Dōgen stressed the central importance of zazen, in which the meditator sits "in a state of brightly alert attention that is free of thoughts, directed to no object, and attached to no particular content." He asserted that Zen is zazen and that to sit zazen is itself enlightenment. Dōgen's writings are forceful, sometimes mystical, and utterly distinctive. "To study the Way," he wrote, "is to study the Self. To study the Self is to forget the self. To forget the self is to be enlightened by all things of the universe."

Robert Frost (1874–1963) was born in San Francisco but lived most of his life in rural New England. Though he cultivated a public persona of the plain-spoken farmer-poet, and in fact never finished a college degree, Frost was as sophisticated an artist as his fellow modernists T. S. Eliot and Ezra Pound. He read widely in Greek and Latin and is perhaps the most skillful verse formalist of the twentieth century. Frost's personal life was marked by impermanence and tragedy. His father, a newspaperman, died of tuberculosis when Frost was eleven, leaving the family destitute; his mother, whose Swedenborgian mysticism was a major influence on her son, died of cancer when Frost was twenty-six. His younger sister Jeanie had to be committed to a mental hospital in 1920, and Frost himself feared at times for his own sanity. Mental illness ran in his family. His daughter Irma was also committed to a mental hospital, and his son Carol committed suicide. Another son died of cholera at age eight, and two of his daughters also died young. Of the poetic process, Frost said, "All I would keep for myself is the freedom of my material—the condition of body and mind now and then to summon aptly from the vast chaos of all I have lived through." He was awarded the Pulitzer Prize four times and attained a popularity unprecedented and still unsurpassed among American poets. He read his poem "The Gift Outright" at the inauguration of John F. Kennedy in 1961.

Jack Gilbert (1925–2012) grew up in Pittsburgh and was educated at the University of Pittsburgh and San Francisco State University. After winning the Yale Younger Poets Prize in 1962, he achieved a degree of fame remarkable for an American poet. Articles about him appeared not just in literary journals but in such glossy magazines as *Esquire*, *Vogue*, and *Glamour*. Gilbert fled the notoriety and spent two decades living in France, Italy, and Greece, publishing infrequently and rarely giving public readings. He was married to the poet Linda Gregg and then to the sculptor Michiko Nogami. In a 2003 interview Gilbert said, "The first influence on my poetry was ancient Chinese poetry—Li Po, Tu Fu—because it had this extraordinary ability to make me experience the emotional thing the poets were feeling, and doing it with no means. I was fascinated by that: how much you could do with so little." He went on to say that poetry is "one of the major ways of keeping the world human. We have almost nothing else, no craft that deals specifically with feeling. . . . Poetry works on the inside of what's happening."

Han Shan ("Cold Mountain"; ninth century) was a legendary poet about whom little is known for certain—even his dates are not known exactly; he may have been born as early as the seventh century. He lived as a hermit on Cold Mountain in the Heaven Terrace Mountain range in southeast China. He carved his poems into the rocks and trees surrounding his hermitage and so identified with Cold Mountain that he took it as his namesake. Han Shan occasionally visited a friend who worked in the kitchen of the local monastery, where he ridiculed the Zen monks for so devoutly pursuing what they already possessed. The monks, in turn, thought Han Shan quite insane. Mostly he wandered alone in the mountains wearing, according to a contemporary memoir by Lu-ch'iu Yin, "a fancy birch-bark hat, a ragged cotton coat, and worn-out sandals." His poems are by turns biting and mystical. Perhaps more than any other poet, Han Shan embodies the freedom of life lived beyond "the floating world" of egoic attachment and human enmeshments. In his book *Rip Rap and Cold Mountain Poems*, Gary Snyder included translations of Han Shan, bringing attention to the ancient poet's work, which would become a major influence on Jack Kerouac and other Beat Generation writers. According to legend, when Han Shan died he walked into a cave in the side of Cold Mountain and "pulled it shut behind him."

Jane Hirshfield (1953–) is a poet, essayist, and translator who grew up in New York City. She received her BA from Princeton University in the school's first graduating class to include women, and she published her first book shortly thereafter in 1973. Hirshfield spent the next eight years focusing on spiritual practice at the San Francisco Zen Center, where she received lay ordination in Soto Zen in 1979. Deeply influenced by both Eastern and Western religious traditions, Hirshfield has edited and translated several collections of spiritual poetry, including *The Ink Dark Moon: Poems by Ono no Komachi and Izumi Shikibu*; *Women of the Ancient Court of Japan*; and *Women in Praise of the Sacred: Forty-Three Centuries of Spiritual Poetry by Women*. Her most recent books of poems are *Given Sugar,*

Given Salt; *Come, Thief*; and *After*. She is also the author of an influential book of essays, *Nine Gates: Entering the Mind of Poetry*. In an interview with *Contemporary Authors*, Hirshfield said, "Poetry, for me, is an instrument of investigation and a mode of perception, a way of knowing and feeling both self and world."

Andrea Hollander (1947–) was born in Berlin to American parents and later raised in Colorado, Texas, New York, and New Jersey. She was educated at Boston University and the University of Colorado. For many years she lived in relative isolation on fifty-two wooded acres in the Ozark Mountains of Arkansas, having little contact with other writers and the larger literary world. She published her first book, *House without a Dreamer*, in 1993 at the age of forty-six. Other volumes include *Woman in the Painting*, *The Other Life*, and *Landscape with Female Figure: New and Selected Poems*. She was writer-in-residence for twenty-two years at Lyon College and currently lives in Portland, Oregon. Of learning the craft of poetry, Hollander has written, "I do not have a degree in creative writing. I learned and continue to learn the craft of writing by studying powerful poems by others. If each such poem is a trick performed by a master magician, I, an aspiring or apprentice magician, must try to figure out how the magic works, and—because no master magician gives away secrets—I must discern this completely on my own."

Kobayashi Issa (1763–1828) was born in the mountain village of Kashiwabara, Japan. His mother died when he was three, a loss that left a lasting wound and profoundly altered the course of his life. When his father remarried and his new wife bore a son, Issa found himself in bitter conflict with his half-brother and stepmother. To ease the tension, his father sent him to Edo (Tokyo) to work as an apprentice when he was just fourteen. As an adult he became a lay priest in the school of Pure Land Buddhism and traveled widely, making his living as a teacher, composing *renga* (linked haiku) with local groups, and correcting verses. He returned to Kashiwabara and nursed his father through his final illness, an experience he recorded in *A Journal of My Father's Last Days*. At fifty-one he married a much younger woman and was briefly happy; but his first son died after a month, a second son died the following year, and a daughter died of smallpox after living just over a year. His wife, Kiku, died after giving birth to a son who himself did not live out the year. Despite or perhaps because of all the loss he suffered, Issa's poems are suffused with a remarkable warmth and empathy, even for the smallest creatures: flies, crickets, fleas, bedbugs, lice. He has been called a Walt Whitman in miniature.

Anna Kamieńska (1920–1986) was a poet, translator, and literary critic who was born in Krasnystaw, Poland. Her father died early, and Kamieńska and her three sisters were brought up by her mother. Beginning in 1937 she studied at the Pedagogical School in Warsaw. During the Nazi occupation she lived in Lublin, and taught in underground village schools. After graduating from college she studied classical philology, initially at the Catholic University of Lublin and then at the University of Lodz. She wrote fifteen books of poetry, two volumes of "Notebooks," three volumes of commentaries on the Bible, and translations from several Slavic languages as well as from Hebrew, Latin, and French. Many of her poems explore the tensions between reason and religious faith.

Jack Kerouac (1922–1969) was born in Lowell, Massachusetts, to French-Canadian parents. With

William Burroughs, Allen Ginsberg, Gary Snyder, Diane di Prima, and others, Kerouac became a leading figure in what would become the Beat Generation. He wrote spontaneously and composed his iconic novel *On the Road* in a series of notebooks, which he then typed out on a continuous reel of paper during three weeks in April 1951. Though known mainly for his novels, Kerouac wrote a great deal of poetry, both haiku and in longer free-verse forms, including his book-length poem, *Mexico City Blues.* Kerouac's interest in Buddhism culminated in a biography of Siddhartha Gautama, *Wake Up*, which was unpublished during his lifetime but eventually serialized in *Tricycle: The Buddhist Review* and published in book form in 2008.

Bill Knott (1940–2014) was born in Carson City, Michigan. Like a number of other poets in this anthology, Knott was orphaned and struggled with mental illness. He spent a year in a mental institution in Elgin, Illinois, when he was fifteen. He worked with his uncle at a farm in Michigan, spent two years in the army, and wrote his first book while working as a hospital orderly. He taught for many years at Emerson College in Boston. His collections include *The Naomi Poems, Book One: Corpse* *and Beans, Becos, Outremer, Laugh at the End of the World: Collected Comic Poems 1969–1999*, and *Stigmata Errata Etcetera*, a collaboration with collages by the artist Star Black.

Yusef Komunyakaa (1947–) was born in Bogalusa, Louisiana, and grew up during the beginnings of the Civil Rights movement. He served in the United States Army during the Vietnam War as a correspondent and as managing editor of the *Southern Cross*. He was awarded a Bronze Star for his service, and his collection *Dien Cai Dau* has been hailed as among the best poems about the Vietnam War. He won the Pulitzer Prize for *Neon Vernacular: New and Selected Poems 1977–1989*. Strongly influenced by jazz, especially the African-American jazz musicians of the 1950s and '60s, Komunyakaa has said, "Jazz has space, and space equals freedom, a place where the wheels of imagination can turn and a certain kind of meditation can take place."

Marilyn Krysl (1942–) grew up in Kansas and Oregon but has lived most of her life in Boulder, Colorado, where she taught for many years at the University of Colorado's MFA program. A practicing Buddhist in the Vipassana tradition, Krysl has dedicated much of her life to service. She has taught English as a second language in the People's Republic of China, volunteered as an unarmed bodyguard for Peace Brigade International in Sri Lanka during the height of the civil war, and tended to the needy at Mother Teresa's Kalighat Home for the Dying Destitutes in Calcutta. She has also worked with those displaced by war in Sudan. She is the author of several books of fiction, including *Dinner with Osama,* and a book of essays, *Yes, There Will Be Singing.* Her most recent book of poetry is *Swear the Burning Vow: Selected and New Poems.* In a 2009 interview she said of her volunteer work, "It's important to me to be able to say, 'I came, I heard, I saw, and I did not turn away. I am still here and I will tell others.'"

Philip Larkin (1922–1985) seems the least likely of poets to be included in an anthology of this kind. He was a decidedly anti-Romantic poet, unspiritual, often glum, often bitingly witty, who famously said, "Deprivation is for me what daffodils were to Wordsworth." Larkin was born Coventry, England. After graduating from Oxford, he began a lifelong career as a librarian, mainly at the University of Hull. In addition to his books of poetry, *The North*

Ship, *The Less Deceived*, *The Whitsun Weddings*, and *High Windows*, Larkin wrote two novels, *Jill* and *A Girl in Winter*, and a book on jazz, *All What Jazz*. He was close friends with the novelist Kingsley Amis, and the protagonist of Amis's *Lucky Jim* is based on Larkin. He was offered but refused the position of Poet Laureate of England. He revealed an intuitive awareness of "no-self" when he described the prospect of making his living as a poet: "If I'd tried in the Forties and Fifties I'd have been a heap of whitened bones long ago. Nowadays you can live by being a poet. A lot of people do it: it means a blend of giving readings and lecturing and spending a year at a university as poet in residence or something. But I couldn't bear that: it would embarrass me very much. I don't want to go around pretending to be me."

D. H. Lawrence (1885–1930) grew up in the coal-mining town of Eastwood, Nottinghamshire, England. His father was a barely literate miner, and his mother, though a teacher, had to do manual labor in a lace factory because of financial difficulties. Much of Lawrence's work can be read as a rebellion against the dehumanizing effects of the Industrial Revolution and the sexual repression of Victorian morality. He suffered official persecution, censorship, and misrepresentation, particularly for the frank sexuality of *Lady Chatterley's Lover,* and spent much of his later life in a voluntary exile, which he called a "savage pilgrimage," in New Mexico. Lawrence was tremendously prolific, writing novels, short stories, poems, plays, essays, travel books, translations, and literary criticism. Though he was known mostly for his novels, his *Complete Poems* runs to over a thousand pages. He was influenced by Ezra Pound, Willam Carlos Williams, and other Imagist poets, and wrote many vivid evocations of the lives of animals and the stark landscape of New Mexico, as well as acerbic poems satirizing what he saw as the moral hypocrisy of Western civilization. His collections of poetry include *Look! We Have Come Through*; *Birds, Beasts, and Flowers*; and *Pansies*, which was banned on publication in England in 1929.

Denise Levertov (1923–1997) was born and grew up in Essex, England. At the age of twelve, she sent some of her poems to T. S. Eliot, who replied with a two-page letter of encouragement. During the Nazi Blitz of London, Levertov served as a civilian nurse. In 1948 she emigrated to America and soon moved beyond her early work in traditional forms, adopting an American idiom and a free verse largely influenced by William Carlos Williams. When the Vietnam War started, Levertov and several other writers founded the Writers and Artists Protest against the War in Vietnam. She participated in antiwar demonstrations and was jailed several times for civil disobedience. She was also a vocal opponent of nuclear weapons and environmental degradation. Her poems encompass both the political horrors of the twentieth century and the mystical dimensions of everyday life. "I saw Paradise," she wrote, "in the dust of the street." Her books include *Here and Now*, *O Taste and See!*, *A Door in the Hive*, and *The Great Unknowing*.

Li Po (701–762) was a legendary figure even during his own lifetime, earning the nickname of "Banished Immortal" and inspiring awe and sometimes fear in those who knew him. Though they only met twice, Tu Fu wrote more than a dozen poems referencing the older and more famous poet. The translator David Hinton writes that Li Po's life was characterized by "wild drinking and a gleeful disdain for decorum." Both his life and poetry appear to have been governed more by spontaneous impulse than adherence to professional ambition or literary convention. As a young man he studied the Confucian classics and became proficient in swordsmanship and other martial arts. His dual nature led him to spend time as a Taoist recluse but also as a kind of "knight errant," righting wrongs inflicted upon the powerless. In this capacity he is thought to have killed several people with his sword. His early life of carefree wandering was disrupted by the An Lushan rebellion. During the war Li Po was imprisoned for two years and briefly exiled. Though he was eventually exonerated, he was greatly weakened, and his wandering lifestyle had to be curtailed in his later years. Hinton regards the spontaneous expression of *tzu-jan*, or "that which is of itself," to be the most essential feature of Li Po's poetry.

Bronisław Maj (1953–) is the author of seven volumes of poetry, which have won him prestigious literary prizes, a reputation as one of the finest poets of his generation, and a place in many anthologies of contemporary poetry published both in Poland and abroad. Maj is also the author of a book about Tadeusz Gajcy, a poet who died during the Warsaw Uprising in 1944. He writes newspaper columns and has edited the literary quarterly *Na Głos* for many years. He lives in Krakow and teaches at the

Jagiellonian University and the School of Creative Writing. The translator Stanisław Barańczak has written of Maj, "In all of his poetry, Bronisław Maj confirms the simple truth that a consistent metaphysical poet cannot, in the final analysis, be anything other than a moralist."

Czesław Miłosz (1911–2004) was born in the village of Szetejnie, Lithuania. He wrote in Polish—he was also fluent in French, English, Lithuanian, and Russian—but considered himself to be both Polish and Lithuanian. "Language," he said, "is the only homeland." He endured World War II in Warsaw and was instrumental in helping Jews in Nazi-occupied Poland, for which he was awarded the medal of the Righteous among the Nations in Yad Vashem, Israel, in 1989. After the war he served as Polish cultural attaché in Paris and defected to the West in 1951. His critical book, *The Captive Mind*, explores the dangers of totalitarianism and offers a searing critique of Soviet Communism. From 1961 to 1998 he was a professor of Slavic languages and literatures at the University of California, Berkeley. Miłosz became a US citizen in 1970 and, after the fall of the Iron Curtain, divided his time between Poland and the United States. He wrote in lonely obscurity for many years; the first book of his poetry to be translated into English did not appear until 1973. Because his books had been banned in Poland, many Polish readers were unaware of him until he was awarded the Nobel Prize in 1980. Discussing the intellectual repression he had witnessed, Miłosz said, "In a room where people unanimously maintain a conspiracy of silence, one word of truth sounds like a pistol shot."

Marianne Moore (1887–1972) was born in Kirkwood, Missouri. Her father suffered a nervous breakdown before she was born and was institutionalized, vanishing from Moore's life. She studied history, law, and politics at Bryn Mawr before turning to poetry. Her early work was praised by T. S. Eliot, Wallace Stevens, William Carlos Williams, Ezra Pound, and other modernist writers. She edited the influential literary magazine *The Dial* from 1925 to 1929, publishing many experimental writers. Like Stevens and Williams, Moore was concerned with the role of the imagination, and in her most famous poem, "Poetry," she called for poets capable of producing "imaginary gardens with real toads in them." In her later years she encouraged younger poets like Allen Ginsberg, John Ashbery, James Merrill, and especially Elizabeth Bishop, with whom she had a lifelong friendship. She lived in Brooklyn and Manhattan for most of her adult life. Though she never traveled to Asia, Moore was deeply influenced by Chinese art. An ardent baseball fan, she threw out the first pitch of the 1968 season in Yankee Stadium. She also wrote the liner notes for Muhammad Ali's spoken word album *I Am the Greatest!* Her *Collected Poems* won the National Book Award, the Pulitzer Prize, and the Bollingen Prize.

Pablo Neruda (1904–1973) was born Neftalí Ricardo Reyes Basoalto (he changed his name to avoid his father's wrath when he started publishing poems) in Parral, a wild region where Neruda grew intimate with the lush forest of central Chile. "I have come out of that landscape," he wrote in his memoir, "that mud, that silence, to roam, to go singing through the world." His father was a railway worker, and his mother, a schoolteacher, died when he was just two months old. Neruda began writing poems early and achieved worldwide fame when he published *Twenty Love Poems and a Song of Despair* (a book for which he was paid five dollars) when he was nineteen. He was strongly influenced by Surrealist poets early in his career but would go on to write in a stunning variety of styles and forms—sonnets, love poems, epic poems about the turbulent history of South America, lacerating political poems, and the earthy, celebratory free verse of the *Elemental Odes*. Neruda was hugely popular, once reading to a crowd of a hundred thousand people in São Paulo. He served as a diplomat in Ceylon, Burma, and Paris, and foreign dignitaries would often greet him by reciting one of his poems. He became a communist and was elected to the senate in 1946. His furious denunciation of President Videla, whom Neruda blamed for a massacre of coal miners, forced him to flee Chile in a daring escape on horseback over the Andes into Argentina. On one occasion Neruda's horse stumbled and fell. His friend Victor Bianchi wrote in his diary, "The wound unleashed the poet's compassion and a moment later, the forest bore witness to the most unexpected scene of tenderness in the midst of our escape. Pablo stroked the horse, smothering it with words of comfort and promising that he wouldn't ride it again for the rest of the journey." Neruda won the Nobel Prize in 1971 but wrote in his *Memoirs* that the greatest honor of his life as a poet was being greeted by a miner who said to him, "Brother, I have known you a long time." He ran for president in Chile, eventually stepping aside for his friend Salvador Allende. In 2013 Neruda's body was exhumed over suspicion that he might have been poisoned by the Pinochet regime, just days after the coup that killed Allende. Evidence was inconclusive. Neruda was hailed by Gabriel García Márquez as "the greatest poet of the twentieth century in any language."

Frank O'Hara (1926–1966), like A. R. Ammons and James Schuyler, served as a sonar operator on a naval destroyer during World War II. He grew up in Grafton, Massachusetts, and went to Harvard on the GI Bill, intending to study music and to pursue a career as a concert pianist, before switching to literature. At Harvard he became friends with John Ashbery, who, along with James Schuyler and Kenneth Koch, would become the central figures of the New York School of poetry. O'Hara was deeply immersed in the art world and counted Jackson Pollock, Willem de Kooning, Joan Mitchell, Larry Rivers, and many other painters among his wide circle of friends. He worked his way up from selling postcards in the gift shop at the Museum of Modern Art to eventually become an assistant curator of painting and sculpture, organizing major shows of Abstract Expressionist art in New York, Spain, and

Italy. He is most famous for his "I-do-this, I-do-that" poems that capture the rush of impressions in Midtown Manhattan. In his mock manifesto, "Personism," O'Hara wrote, "I'm not saying that I don't have practically the most lofty ideas of anyone writing today, but what difference does that make? They're just ideas. The only good thing about it is that when I get lofty enough I've stopped thinking and that's when refreshment arrives."

Alicia Ostriker (1937–) is a poet, critic, and activist who was born in New York City and educated at Brandeis University and the University of Wisconsin–Madison. Twice a finalist for the National Book Award, Ostriker has published numerous volumes of poetry, including *The Book of Seventy*, *No Heaven*, and *The Volcano Sequence*. She has also written several volumes of criticism and biblical commentary, including *Feminist Revision and the Bible* and *For the Love of God: The Bible as an Open Book*. She taught for many years at Rutgers University. Of her creative process, Ostriker has said, "When I write a poem, I am crawling into the dark. Or else I am an aperture. Something needs to be put into language, and it chooses me. I invite such things. 'Not I, not I, but the wind that blows through me,' as D. H. Lawrence says. I write as an American, a woman, a Jew, a mother, a wife, a lover of beauty and art, a teacher, an idealist, a skeptic."

Ron Padgett (1942–) was born in Tulsa, Oklahoma. As a high school student, Padgett cofounded the avant-garde journal *White Dove Review*, publishing poems by Allen Ginsberg, Robert Creeley, Jack Kerouac, e.e. cummings, Amiri Baraka, and other prominent experimental poets. In 1960 he moved to New York City to attend Columbia University, and in 1965 spent a year in Paris on a Fulbright scholarship studying and translating French poetry. He eventually made his home in New York City's East Village, where he taught poetry classes at St. Mark's Church and became friends with John Ashbery, James Schuyler, Kenneth Koch, and other poets and painters associated with the New York School. He has published, in addition to his own books of poems, translations of Blaise Cendrars and Guillaume Apollinaire, edited the *Collected Works of Joe Brainard*, and written widely on education, including *The Teachers and Writers Handbook of Poetic Forms*, which he edited. His book *How Long* won the 2013 *Los Angeles Times* Book Award for poetry. Witty, playful, and restlessly inventive,

Padgett's poems absorb a wide range of influences, from French Surrealist and Dadaist poets to the Marx Brothers, Red Skelton, and the Three Stooges.

Lucia Perillo (1958–2016) grew up in the suburbs of New York City and graduated from McGill University in Montreal, where she studied wildlife management. She subsequently worked at the Denver Wildlife Research Center and at the San Francisco Bay Wildlife Refuge, leading nature tours. She completed her MA in English at Syracuse University, while working seasonally as a park ranger at Mount Rainier National Park in Washington state. Her science background and intimate knowledge of plants and animals inform much of her poetry. She also published a book of essays, *I Have Heard the Vultures Singing: Field Notes on Poetry, Illness, and Nature*, and a book of short stories, *Happiness Is a Chemical in the Brain*. In both her poetry and prose, she wrote with extraordinary candor about living with multiple sclerosis. Her book of poems *On the Spectrum of Possible Deaths* (2012) was a finalist for the National Book Award. She taught at Syracuse University, Southern Illinois University, and in the Warren Wilson MFA program.

Fernando Pessoa (1888–1935) was born in Lisbon, Portugal. His father died of tuberculosis when Pessoa was five years old, and his younger brother died the following year. The family moved with his mother's new husband, a consul, to Durban, South Africa, where Pessoa attended an English school. He returned to Portugal in 1905 and lived the rest of his life there. He studied briefly at the University of Lisbon and began to publish criticism, prose, and poetry soon thereafter while working as a commercial translator. Though he wrote voluminously, Pessoa published very little during his lifetime. He appears to have had an inherent sense of the Buddhist concept of emptiness, regarding the self as a fluid, dynamic construction. He wrote most of his poems from three personas, or heteronyms, as he called them—distinctive poetic voices, each with a unique style and an invented biography: Alberto Caeiro, a pastoral, philosophical free-verse poet; Ricardo Reis, a physician who wrote formal odes in the style of Horace; and Álvaro de Campos, an expansive, Whitmanesque poet and London-based naval engineer. (These personas knew of and occasionally voiced opinions about one another's work.) The Nobel Prize–winner José Saramago wrote a novel based on one of Pessoa's heteronyms: *The Year* *of the Death of Ricardo Reis.* John Ashbery has called Pessoa "one of the great twentieth-century poets, the equal of Yeats, Rilke, Valery, Lorca, Pasternak, or Hart Crane."

Paulann Petersen (1942–) was born in Portland, Oregon, into a nonliterary, blue-collar family. She recalls that there wasn't a single book of poetry in her childhood home. Petersen attended Pomona College in California and was later a Stegner Fellow at Stanford University. She taught high school for many years in Klamath Falls and Portland, Oregon, and went on to become Oregon's sixth poet laureate. An ecstatic poet in the tradition of Walt Whitman, Rumi, and Pablo Neruda, Petersen's books include *The Wild Awake, The Voluptuary,* and *Understory.* Of the beauty and variety of her home state, Petersen has written, "Oregon is mountains, ocean, high desert, rain forest. It's the hot springs in Hart Mountain Antelope Refuge, the Church of Elvis in downtown Portland, pelicans on Klamath Lake, herons in Oaks Bottom on the Willamette. Oregon is abundance, variety vast and gorgeous. It teaches me inclusiveness and gratitude. Oregon encourages a wide embrace."

Po Chü-i (772–846) was born during the Middle T'ang period, a time of rebuilding after the An Lushan rebellion and just a few years after the passing of three major poets of the era, Li Po, Tu Fu, and Wang Wei. Po Chü-i began his career as a minor official, eventually becoming governor of three different provinces. He was deeply immersed in the study of Zen, and his poems exemplify the clarity, simplicity, and depth of wisdom so valued in the Chinese poetic tradition. The translator David Hinton suggests that Po Chü-i's poetry joins "the intimacies of a full heart and the distances of an empty mind."

Ezra Pound (1885–1972) was born in Hailey, Idaho, and went on to become one of the twentieth century's most cosmopolitan and controversial poets. He was enormously influential early in his career, championing the work of Robert Frost, T. S. Eliot, William Carlos Williams, and others, and offering literary declarations: "Make it new!" "Poetry is news that stays news." "The image is more than an idea. It is a vortex or cluster of fused ideas and is endowed with energy." Indeed, Pound's impact was first felt in his development of Imagism, a movement that was both a reaction against Victorian rhetorical and decorative excess and an infusion of the clarity, precision, and economy of language of the ancient Chinese and Japanese poetry Pound was translating. His "version" (or loose translation) of Li Po's "The River Merchant's Wife" has become a classic. Pound moved to Italy in 1924, and throughout the 1930s and 1940s was a vocal supporter of both Mussolini and Hitler. He made hundreds of radio broadcasts during World War II denouncing the United States, Franklin Roosevelt, usury, and the Jews. He was arrested by American forces in 1945, charged with treason, and spent several months in a prison camp in Pisa, where he began work on his epic poem, *The Cantos.* On his return to the States, he was deemed unfit to stand trial and spent twelve years in St. Elizabeth's psychiatric hospital in Washington, DC, until Frost, Ernest Hemingway, and other prominent writers secured his release. Pound later recanted his anti-Semitic views, but many critics and readers never forgave him, and his winning of the Bollingen Prize in 1949 sparked a fierce controversy. His major works include *Ripostes*, *Hugh Selwyn Mauberley*, and the *Cantos.*

Jacques Prévert (1900–1977) was a poet and screenwriter who was born in Neuilly-sur-Seine and grew up in Paris. He was called up for military service in 1918 and after the war sent to defend French interests in the Near East. Prévert participated actively in the Surrealist movement and belonged to a group of writers and artists that included Marcel Duchamp, Raymond Queneau, Pablo Picasso, Alberto Giacometti, and Yves Tanguy. He was also a member of the agitprop theatrical group Octobre. Prévert wrote a number of screenplays for the director Marcel Carne, including *Port of Shadows, The Night Visitors*, and the highly acclaimed *Children of Paradise*. Several of his poems were set to music, most notably "Autumn Leaves," which enjoyed a wide popularity and was recorded by Edith Piaf, Johnny Mercer, and Nat King Cole.

Kenneth Rexroth (1905–1982) was a poet, painter, translator, and essayist who was born in South Bend, Indiana, to an alcoholic father and a chronically ill mother. His mother died when he was eleven and his father died just three years later, after which Rexroth went to live with his aunt in Chicago. There he became involved in radical leftist politics and enrolled in the Art Institute of Chicago. He traveled widely as a young man throughout the United States, Mexico, South America, and Europe before settling for good in San Francisco. He was largely self-taught (Rexroth scorned institutional education, calling universities "fog factories") and wrote a weekly "great books" column for the *Saturday Review* on Homer, Lady Murasaki, Cervantes, Shakespeare, Tolstoy, and others. A practicing Buddhist, Rexroth was instrumental in heightening American awareness of ancient Chinese and Japanese poetry through his translations, his own poetry—he was one of the first American poets to write haiku—as well as his influence on Gary Snyder, Allen Ginsberg, Lawrence Ferlinghetti, and other Beat poets. Though he resisted the label, Rexroth has been called the "father of the Beats." An academic critic once suggested that he belonged, with Gary Snyder and Philip Whalen, to the "bear-shit-on-the-trail school of poetry," which Rexroth took as a compliment.

Yannis Ritsos (1909–1990), like many of the poets represented in this anthology, suffered tremendous losses early in life. He was born into wealth, but his family suffered financial catastrophe that led to both his father and sister going insane. His mother and an older brother died of tuberculosis, and Ritsos himself had to be confined to a sanatorium in Athens from 1927 to 1931 with the disease. He joined the Communist Party of Greece in 1931, and when the right-wing dictator Ioannis Metaxas came to power in 1936, Ritsos's landmark book *Epitaphios* was burned on the steps of the Acropolis. During the Axis occupation, Ritsos joined the Greek resistance and supported the left during the subsequent civil war (1946–1949), which resulted in his being imprisoned from 1948 to 1952. The poems included in this anthology are from *Diaries in Exile*, which Ritsos wrote between 1948 and 1950 while a political prisoner first on the island of Limnos and then at the infamous camp on the desert island Makronisos. His books were banned several times in Greece, and in 1967 he was arrested by the Papadopolous dictatorship and sent to a prison camp in Gyarous. He was proposed nine times for the Nobel Prize and was awarded the Lenin Peace Prize in 1956.

Kay Ryan (1945–) was born in San Jose, California, and grew up in the San Joaquin Valley and the Mojave Desert, landscapes reflected in the pared-down style of her poetry. Writing in obscurity for many years, Ryan gained a wide audience when she was named United States Poet Laureate in 2008. In 2011 she was awarded a MacArthur Fellowship and won the Pulitzer Prize for her book *The Best of It: New and Selected Poems*. Witty, playful, and incisive, her poetry takes on existential questions and often has a parable-like quality that is distinctive in contemporary American poetry. In an interview with *The Paris Review,* she said, "With my work, you have to always think there's a smidgen of laughter in it, however sad it might be, however lonely or lost. If you feel worse after you've read it, then I've failed."

Ryōkan (1758–1831) is one of Japan's most beloved poets. He was also a master calligrapher. His childhood name was Eizo, but when he decided to become a monk in 1777 at the Sōtō Zen temple Kōshō-ji, he took the name Ryōkan Taigu. *Ryo* means "good," *kan* suggests "large-heartedness," and *Taigu* means "great fool"—qualities that are immediately apparent in his poetry. More literally, "Ryōkan" may also refer to an inn. Ryōkan attained *satori* while at Entsū-ji and received *inka* from his teacher, Kokusen. He lived much of the rest of his life as a hermit, though his fondness for children and laborers is well known. Many stories attest to his playfulness, generosity, and charming eccentricities. When a famous scholar, Kameda Hosai, visited him, they spent the day talking poetry and Zen. Ryōkan decided to go to the village to get sake so they might continue their discussion into the evening. Hosai waited and waited, but Ryōkan did not return. Finally, Hosai set out to find the poet and discovered him sitting under a pine tree, enraptured by the full moon. Hosai shouted, "Ryōkan! Where have you been? I've been waiting for more than three hours! I thought something terrible had happened to you!" Ryōkan replied, "Hosai-san! You have come just in time. Isn't the moon splendid?"

Saigyō (1118–1190) was born in Kyoto into the Sato branch of the powerful Fujiwara clan, during the tumultuous transition from the old court nobles to the new samurai warriors. Saigyō wanted to follow the family tradition and become a samurai, and by the age of eighteen he was captain of the Emperor Toba's palace guard, highly skilled in archery, horseback riding, and other military arts. But for reasons still unclear—possibly because of sexual scandal or a romantic involvement with a woman of higher social rank—he abruptly left court life at twenty-three. In 1140 he became a wandering Buddhist monk, living in the mountains as a hermit and taking long, poetic journeys to northern Honshū that would inspire, nearly five centuries later, Bashō's *Narrow Road to the Deep North*.

Saigyō was a master of *waka*, a five-line form that follows a 5-7-5-7-7 syllabic pattern.

James Schuyler (1923–1991), along with Frank O'Hara, Kenneth Koch, John Ashbery, and Barbara Guest, was a central member of the New York School of poets. He was born in Chicago but grew up in Washington, DC, and East Aurora, New York. After serving as a sonar man on a destroyer during World War II, he attended Bethany College in West Virginia but did not graduate, claiming that he spent more time "playing bridge" than studying. Schuyler spent two years in Rome working as a secretary for W. H. Auden. He then moved to New York City in 1950 and lived for a time with O'Hara and Ashbery. Like them, Schuyler was immersed in the art world; he wrote for *Art News* and became a curator of circulating exhibitions at the Museum of Modern Art. Schuyler's personal life was marked by financial stress and mental illness—he suffered a series of psychotic breaks and had to be repeatedly hospitalized—which made him increasingly reclusive in his later years. Unlike his fellow New York School poets, Schuyler was largely a pastoral poet, observing the changing weather and seasons with a scrupulous and tenderhearted attention—what he called "the pure pleasure of simply looking"—reminiscent of ancient Chinese poetry. In his long poem "Hymn to Life" Schuyler writes, "And there the Lincoln Memorial crumbles. It looks so solid: it won't / Last. The impermanence of permanence, is that all there is?" He won the Pulitzer Prize in 1980 for his book *The Morning of the Poem*.

William Shakespeare (1564–1616) was born in Stratford-upon-Avon. His father, John Shakespeare, was an alderman and glover, and his mother, Mary Arden, came from an affluent landowning family. Little is known about Shakespeare's personal or professional life. He began his career as an actor—still a somewhat disreputable profession in the late 1500s, a fact to which Shakespeare refers in Sonnet 110 when he writes: "Alas! 'tis true, I have gone here and there / and made myself a motley to the view"—and was writer, actor, and part-owner of a theater company called the King's Men. A number of the sonnets deal with impermanence and the passage of time, a theme that preoccupied poets during the Renaissance. He also understood the relationship between what the Buddha called form and emptiness. In *A Midsummer Night's Dream*, the character of Theseus speaks of poetry: "The poet's eye, in a fine frenzy rolling, / doth glance from heaven to Earth, from Earth to heaven; / and as imagination bodies forth the forms of things unknown, / the poet's pen turns them to shape, and gives to airy nothings / a local habitation and a name."

Old Shōju (aka Shōju-rojin 1642–1721) was one of the most eminent Zen masters of Japan, a strict disciplinarian who hurled insults and blows at his students in an effort to free them from their self-centeredness. He is known today for his poems and for the influence he exerted on Hakuin Ekaku, who almost single-handedly revived the Rinzai school of Zen Buddhism.

Tracy K. Smith (1972–) was born in Falmouth, Massachusetts. She grew up in Northern California and earned degrees from Harvard and Columbia Universities. She won the Pulitzer Prize for *Life on Mars* and the National Book Award for *Ordinary Light*. In an interview with *Ploughshares*, Smith spoke of the role of joy in her poetry: "Joy is a part of my process. In fact, I'd go so far as to say that poetry, as a practice, necessitates a sense of joy. . . . And a real sense of play and abandon—even when we are relying on hard-won technique, and even when the aim is deadly serious. How often do we get the excuse to stop, think, and then stop thinking altogether and try to listen to what sits behind or outside of our thoughts? Poets are lucky."

Gary Snyder (1930–) is a poet, translator, environmental activist, and America's preeminent Buddhist poet. He was born in San Francisco and grew up in Washington state and Portland, Oregon. He graduated from Reed College with a degree in literature and anthropology, reflecting an interest in native peoples that has spanned his entire career. Following college, Snyder spent his summers working as a timber scaler at Warm Springs Indian Reservation and as a fire lookout on Crater Mountain and Sourdough Mountain in the North Cascades. In 1955 Snyder traveled to Kyoto to study Zen and spent much of the next twelve years there. With Philip Whalen, Allen Ginsberg, Jack Kerouac, and Gregory Corso, Snyder was a central member of the Beat poets; the character of Japhy Ryder in Kerouac's novel *Dharma Bums* is based on Snyder. He has been instrumental in widening the readership for ancient Chinese and Japanese Zen poetry in America. His first book, *Riprap and Cold Mountain Poems*, includes translations of the T'ang Dynasty recluse poet Han Shan. Other works include *Myths and Texts, Turtle Island* (winner of the Pulitzer Prize), *Mountains and Rivers without End*, and *No Nature: New and Selected Poems.* In a recent essay Snyder discussed the relationship between poetry and meditation: "Traditions of deliberate attention to consciousness, and of making poems, are as old as humankind. Meditation looks inward, poetry holds forth. One is private, the other is out in the world. One enters the moment, the other shares it. But in practice it is never entirely clear which is doing which."

Ikkyū Sojun (1394–1481) was an iconoclastic Zen monk and poet. He was born in a small suburb of Kyoto, the illegitimate son of Emperor Go-Komatsu and a low-ranking court noblewoman. At the age of five he was placed in a Rinzai Zen temple in Kyoto, where he first studied Chinese poetry. Ikkyū is one of the most engaging and eccentric figures in the history of Zen. To Japanese children he is a folk hero: a bit of a trickster, always outwitting his teachers and the shogun. He abhorred the hierarchy he found in the Zen monasteries of his day, and when he was offered a certificate of enlightenment he rejected it. He believed that the sacred could be accessed in ordinary, secular life through the practice of mindfulness. He left the monastery and became a wandering monk, taking the nickname Crazy Cloud and teaching the dharma to hobos, criminals, and prostitutes. Ikkyū held some highly unconventional views. He argued that his enlightenment was deepened by consorting with pavilion girls, considered sexual intercourse a religious rite, and could be seen entering brothels wearing his black monk's robes. "The autumn breeze of a single night of love," he said, "is better than a hundred thousand years of sitting meditation."

William Stafford (1914–1993) was born in Hutchinson, Kansas. The family had to move frequently during the Depression for his father to find work, and Stafford helped out by delivering newspapers, working in the sugar beet fields, and as an electrician's apprentice. Stafford's ethical principles showed early in his life when he defied segregation policies at the University of Kansas by sitting with African-American students in the cafeteria. A Quaker and committed pacifist, one of "the quiet of the land," he registered as a conscientious objector during World War II and worked in Civilian Public Service camps in Arkansas, California, and Illinois, which he wrote about in his memoir *Down in My Heart*. His first book of poems, *West of Your City*, did not appear until he was forty-six. His second book, *Traveling through the Dark*, won the National Book Award in 1963. In his book of essays, *Writing the Australian Crawl*, Stafford said, "A writer is not so much someone who has something to say as he is someone who has found a process that will bring about new things he would not have thought of if he hadn't started to say them."

Wallace Stevens (1879–1955) was born in Reading, Pennsylvania. Stevens studied law at Harvard and New York Law School, graduating in 1903. After working for several law firms in New York City, he joined the Hartford Accident and Indemnity Company in Hartford, Connecticut, where he would spend the rest of his career and rise to the position of vice president. As a young man Stevens was involved in the modernist revolutions taking place in all the arts, beginning with the Armory Show of international art in 1913. He was strongly influenced by the paintings of Paul Klee, Paul Cézanne, and Pablo Picasso. Stevens was familiar with Buddhist ideas; he read *The Essence of Buddha's Teaching,* a pamphlet prepared by Nyanatiloka, the eminent scholar-monk, as well as works by Max Mueller, the leading Orientalist of the day. Stevens's poetry explores the tensions between reality and imagination and the role of poetry in a world disinhabited by God. In his poem "The Man with the Blue Guitar," he wrote that "Poetry / Exceeding music must take the place / Of empty heaven and its hymns, / Ourselves in poetry must take their place." His first book, *Harmonium*, appeared in 1923 when Stevens was forty-four. He went on to win the Bollingen Prize, the National Book Award, and the Pulitzer Prize.

Ruth Stone (1915–2011) was born in Roanoke, Virginia, but lived most of her adult life in rural Vermont. She began writing poetry at the age of five and never stopped. She attended the University of Illinois at Urbana-Champaign and published her first book of poetry, *In an Iridescent Time*, in 1959. Soon afterward her second husband, the poet and writer Walter Stone, committed suicide, leaving her to raise three young children alone. His death would haunt Stone's poetry for the rest of her life; she described her books as "love poems, all written to a dead man." She worked in relative obscurity for much of her life but was greatly honored in her later years, winning the National Book Critics Circle Award for *Ordinary Life* in 1999 and the National Book Award for *In the Next Galaxy* in 2002.

Su Tung P'o (1037–1101) was a poet, painter, calligrapher, and statesman, and is regarded as the greatest poet of the Song Dynasty (960–1279). He was born in Meishan in what is now Sichuan province, into a highly literary family—his father and brother were renowned writers. Su was educated by a Taoist priest and by his mother. He performed so brilliantly on the civil service exams—answering questions on the Confucian classics—that he attracted the attention of Emperor Renzong. He went on to have an influential career in government but was twice exiled over political disputes and lived much of his life as a subsistence farmer. The translator David Hinton writes, "Rather than consciousness giving shape to the world it encounters, Su's poems enact consciousness wandering like water, the operant metaphor for the Tao, taking shape according to what it encounters. . . . And in spite of the considerable hardship and political frustration he suffered, this weaving together of consciousness into the fabric of wilderness allowed Su a detachment and emotional balance, even lightheartedness, that has endured as part of the Chinese cultural legend."

Anna Swir (1909–1984) was born in Warsaw, Poland, to an artistic though impoverished family.

She worked from an early age, supporting herself while attending university to study medieval Polish literature. In the 1930s she worked for a teachers' association and began publishing poetry. Swir joined the resistance during World War II and served as a military nurse during the Warsaw Uprising; at one point she came within an hour of being executed before she was spared. In addition to writing poetry, Swir wrote plays and stories for children and directed a children's theater. She lived in Krakow from 1945 until her death from cancer in 1984. Like Wisława Szymborska, Czesław Miłosz, and other Polish writers, Swir's poetry was strongly influenced by her experience of the war. In 1974 she published *Building the Barricade*, which describes the suffering that she both witnessed and experienced herself during the Nazi occupation. Swir has also written eloquently about the female body in various stages of life in *Talking to My Body*.

Wisława Szymborska (1923–2012) was born in Prowent, Poland, but her family moved to Warsaw when she was eight, and she spent the rest of her life there. She began writing poetry at the age of four. Like Czesław Miłosz and many other Polish writers, she witnessed the horrors of World War II and endured the brutal collectivism of the Soviet occupation, both of which profoundly influenced her poetry. After the Nazis invaded Poland in September 1939, Szymborska worked as a railway clerk to avoid deportation to Germany as a forced laborer. During that time she took classes at illegal underground universities. After the war she studied Polish literature and sociology at Jagiellonian University, and worked as an editor and columnist. Though she became a member of the Communist Party in 1952 and supported socialist themes in her early work, even writing a poem to Lenin, she later disavowed her first two books of political poetry. In the late 1950s she began to befriend dissidents, joining their demands for freedom of speech. She compared Josef Stalin to the abominable snowman in the 1957 poem "Calling Out to Yeti," and her poetry frequently undermines collectivist abstractions and grand political themes in favor of the individual and the ordinary/extraordinary objects and events of daily life. Her poems are both playful and philosophical, transparent and complex. Szymborska became hugely popular in Poland. The Polish rock singer Kora turned her poem "Nothing Twice" into a hit song, and her poem "Love at First Sight" inspired the enigmatic film *Red* by the Polish director Krzysztof Kieślowski.

In awarding her the Nobel Prize in 1996, the committee called Szymborska a "Mozart of poetry."

Tomas Tranströmer (1931–2015) was born in Stockholm, Sweden, and raised by his mother, a schoolteacher, following her divorce from his father. He began writing poetry in high school and published his first book when he was twenty-three. He took a degree in psychology from Stockholm University, where he also studied history, religion, and literature. For many years he divided his time between writing and translating poetry and working as a psychologist at the Roxtuna center for juvenile offenders. He suffered a stroke in 1990 that rendered him partially paralyzed and unable to speak, though he continued to write and publish. He was awarded the Nobel Prize in 2011. Deeply tied to the landscapes and seasonal cycles of Scandinavia, Tranströmer's work carries forward the currents of early twentieth-century Surrealist poetry as well as much older mystical traditions. Writing in the *Boston Review*, the critic Katie Peterson observed that Tranströmer "has perfected a particular kind of epiphanic lyric . . . in which nature is the active, energizing subject, and the self (if the self is present at all) is the object."

Tu Fu (712–770), often referred to as China's "poet-historian" or "poet-sage," is one of China's greatest poets. Tu Fu experienced impermanence early in his life. His mother died shortly after he was born, and an older brother died young. He was born during the T'ang Dynasty, China's cultural golden age, but the peace of the period was disrupted by the An Lushan rebellion and the cataclysmic civil war it sparked in 755. Tu Fu agonized over the violence and upheaval—nearly two-thirds of China's population was either killed or displaced during the war—and he was forced to move repeatedly to keep his family safe. Because of the strife and his troubled relationship to court politics, Tu Fu was largely exiled from the center of Chinese culture and spent much of his later life as a kind of wandering recluse. But he saw the turmoil in China as emblematic of a human drama subsumed by natural processes: "The nation falls into ruins; mountains and rivers continue."

Wei Ying-Wu (737–792) is considered one of the greatest poets of the T'ang Dynasty. Like Tu Fu and Li Po, Wei lived through China's convulsive An Lushan rebellion, which devastated the country and left his own family in ruins. The external upheaval and loss of his aristocratic position turned

Wei to a more contemplative, reclusive life, though he also held various government positions and was strongly motivated to alleviate the suffering of those displaced and impoverished by war. The collapse of China's cultural magnificence suffuses Wei's work with a sense of loss and melancholy, but the translator David Hinton suggests that in Wei's poems "loss and absence often seem indistinguishable from the emptiness of enlightenment."

Walt Whitman (1819–1892) was born in Huntington, Long Island, New York. The family moved to Brooklyn when Whitman was four and, except for a year in New Orleans and several years in Washington, DC, during the war, he lived there his entire life, until poor health necessitated a move to Camden, New Jersey. Whitman taught school briefly and not very successfully; he made his living mainly as a printer, reporter, and newspaper editor. He self-published the first edition of *Leaves of Grass* and helped promote the book by producing several anonymous self-reviews, all quite positive. Despite his efforts, the book was either ignored or scorned for its frank sexuality and the unconventional nature of the verse—Whitman was the first poet to wholly abandon traditional rhyme and meter, employing instead flowing biblical cadences and chantlike repetitions. He was deeply influenced by Emerson; Whitman said, "I was simmering, simmering, simmering. Emerson brought me to a boil." After reading his poetry, Henry David Thoreau asked Whitman if he knew the sacred texts of the East. Whitman replied, "No, tell me about them." But in his assertion of the unity and divinity of all existence and his leveling of artificial hierarchies, Whitman's poetry resonates with the wisdom streams of Taoism and Buddhism, which he may have intuited, or absorbed through Emerson. He appears to have had a mystical experience sometime in the early 1850s, which transformed his poetry from the conventional, mediocre verse he was writing to the soaring, visionary, utterly distinctive poetry of "Song of Myself." For a poet who prized union so highly, the Civil War was an anguishing experience. Whitman spent three years visiting wounded and dying soldiers in the hospitals in and around Washington, DC. He brought gifts to the soldiers, wrote letters for those who were illiterate or too weak to write, sat with them as they died, and offered comfort to all who needed it, both Union and Confederate, black and white. He wrote about his wartime experiences in *Drum-Taps* and *Specimen Days*. "Those three years," he said, "I consider the greatest privilege and satisfaction, (with all their feverish excitements and physical deprivations and lamentable sights) and, of course, the most profound lesson of my life. I can say that in my ministerings I comprehended all whoever came in my way, northern or southern, and slighted none. It arous'd and brought out and decided undream'd-of depths of emotion." More than any other American poet, Whitman approached the ideal of the bodhisattva.

William Carlos Williams (1883–1963) was born in Rutherford, New Jersey, and he lived his whole life there, apart from his years at the University of Pennsylvania, where he studied medicine and became friends with Ezra Pound. He became a family doctor, tending primarily to poor Italian and Polish immigrants, making house calls, calming fevers, and delivering babies at all hours, often without pay. He was a central figure in the modernist revolution and sought to strip language clean of its encrusted poetic associations and to speak in a distinctively American idiom. He rejected what he saw as the disillusionment and cultural elitism of T. S. Eliot, and he tried to bring poetry closer to lived experience. "No ideas but in things," he wrote, and many of his poems have a hard, clear, Zenlike quality. Though he had to pay for the publication of his first four books, he went on to win both the National Book Award and the Pulitzer Prize, and is recognized as one of the great poets of the twentieth century.

William Wordsworth (1770–1850) was born in Cockermouth, in the Lake District of Northwest England. He attended St. John's College, Cambridge, where he was a mediocre student, receiving the equivalent of a "gentleman's C." In 1790 he took a walking tour of Europe and explored the Alps extensively, an experience that he wrote about in his autobiographical epic poem *The Prelude or, Growth of a Poet's Mind*. Wordsworth greeted the French Revolution and its promise of individual rights and social equality with great enthusiasm. In 1798 he and his friend Samuel Taylor Coleridge published *Lyrical Ballads*, itself a revolutionary document, a fierce rejection of the dominant conception of poetry of the time, the eighteenth-century emphasis on wit, reason, lofty subjects, and elevated poetic diction. He also rejected the tight rhymed couplets of Pope and Dryden in favor of a Miltonic blank verse as well as sonnets, ballads, and odes. In the *Preface to the Lyrical Ballads*, published in the second edition in 1801, Wordsworth articulated a new sensibility in poetry and ushered in the age of Romanticism. He called for poems that dealt with real life, rather than conventional poetic themes, in a "language really used by men." In the *Preface* Wordsworth gave his famous definition of poetry as "the spontaneous overflow of powerful feelings: it takes its origin from emotion recollected in tranquility."

James Wright (1927–1980) was born in Martins Ferry, Ohio, to working-class parents, neither of whom attended school beyond the eighth grade. His early life was marked by poverty and a nervous breakdown that would force him to miss a year of high school. He served in the army in Japan during the American occupation and then attended Kenyon College, where he studied with John Crowe Ransom and later with Theodore Roethke and Stanley Kunitz at the University of Washington. Wright's emotional life was extremely challenging. He suffered depression and bipolar disorder and struggled with alcoholism. He had to be hospitalized on several occasions and was subjected to electroshock therapy. Like many other poets of his generation, Wright broke from the conventional rhyme and meter of his early work and found his voice in a more open-ended, imagistic free verse of *The Branch Will Not Break* and

Shall We Gather at the River. With his friend Robert Bly, he translated German and South American poets and was deeply influenced by ancient Chinese and Japanese poetry, influences he brought to bear with brilliant effect on poems about the postindustrial wasteland of the American Midwest. He won the Pulitzer Prize in 1972 for his *Collected Poems.*

William Butler Yeats (1865–1939) was born in Dublin, Ireland, and educated there and in London. He spent childhood holidays in County Sligo and was influenced by both the landscape and the folklore of that place. Like Neruda, Yeats was deeply involved in politics, and served as an Irish senator for two terms. Yeats also had a lifelong interest in mystical pursuits, including Spiritualism, Theosophy, séances, astrology, Hermeticism, automatic writing, and the occult. He was a seeker of ultimate truths, asserting that "talent perceives differences; genius, unity." In his book *A Vision* he developed a mystical system to explain his theories of physical and spiritual masks and the cycles of life. In 1923 he was awarded the Nobel Prize in literature for what the Nobel committee described as "inspired poetry, which in a highly artistic form gives expression to the spirit of a whole nation." Yeats famously likened the poetic process to a lover's quarrel with oneself: "We make out of the quarrel with others, rhetoric, but of the quarrel with ourselves, poetry."

Adam Zagajewski (1945–) was born in Lwów, Poland, but his family was expelled by the Ukrainians to central Poland in 1946. He lived in Berlin for several years, moved to France in 1982, and has taught at universities in the United States, including the University of Houston and the University of Chicago. Considered one of the Generation of '68 or New Wave writers in Poland, Zagajewski wrote protest poetry early in his career, though his later work is more lyrical. The poet and critic Robert Pinsky observed that Zagajewski's poems are "about the presence of the past in ordinary life: history not as chronicle of the dead, or an anima to be illuminated by some doctrine, but as an immense, sometimes subtle force inhering in what people see and feel every day—and in the ways we see and feel."

Credits

Dick Allen, "Listening Deeply" from *The Zen Master Poems*. Copyright © 2016 by Richard Allen. Reprinted with the permission of Wisdom Publications.

A. R. Ammons, "Continuing" and "In Memoriam Mae Noblitt" from *A Coast of Trees*. Copyright © 1981 by A. R. Ammons. "The City Limits" from *The Selected Poems, Expanded Edition*. Copyright © 1971 by A. R. Ammons. "Old Geezer" from *Brink Road*. Copyright © 1996 by A. R. Ammons. "Clarifications," "Reflective," and "Stills" from *The Really Short Poems of A. R. Ammons*. Copyright © 1990 by A. R. Ammons. All poems reprinted with the permission of W. W. Norton and Company, Inc.

Matsuo Bashō, "Wrapping the rice cakes" and "A cicada shell," translated by Robert Hass, from *The Essential Haiku: Versions of Basho, Buson and Issa*,

Anna Kamieńska. Reprinted with the permission of the translators and Paraclete Press.

Jack Kerouac, "In my medicine cabinet" from *Book of Haikus* by Jack Kerouac, edited by Regina Weinreich. Copyright © 2003 by The Estate of Stella Kerouac, John Sampas, Literary Representative. Used by permission of Penguin Books, an imprint of Penguin Publishing Group, a division of Penguin Random House LLC.

Bill Knott, "Death" from *Laugh at the End of the World: Collected Comic Poems 1969–1999.* Copyright © 2000 by Bill Knott. Reprinted with the permission of The Permissions Company, Inc., on behalf of BOA Editions Ltd., www.boaeditions.org.

Yusef Komunyakaa, "Facing It" from *Neon Vernacular: New and Selected Poems.* Copyright © 1993 by Yusef Komunyakaa. Reprinted with permission of Wesleyan University Press.

Marilyn Krysl, "She Speaks a Various Language" from *What We Have to Live With* by Marilyn Krysl.

Acknowledgments

I bow to Josh Bartok and everyone at Wisdom Publications for their skill and care in bringing this book into the world. I am deeply grateful to Suntara Loba and the Max and Anna Levinson Foundation for a generous grant in support of this project. For their encouragement, enthusiasm, and helpful suggestions, I am indebted to my students at Lighthouse Writers Workshop and Mountain Writers Series. For the blessing of their friendship and support, I am grateful to John Kadlecek, Harriet Stratton, Ed and Sue Einowski, Andrea Hollander, Satya Byock, and Fred Muratori. And to my Dharma teachers, John Ankele, Peter Williams, and Larry Christensen, I made this book with you in mind. My wife, Alice Boyd, provided invaluable help with everything from editorial decisions to manuscript preparation, and reminded me throughout of the true connection between mindfulness and joy.

About the Editor

 John Brehm is the author of two award-winning books of poems, *Help Is on the Way* and *Sea of Faith*, and the associate editor of *The Oxford Book of American Poetry*. His poems have appeared in *Poetry*, *The Southern Review*, *New Ohio Review*, *The Sun*, *The Gettysburg Review*, *Gulf Coast*, *The Writer's Almanac*, the *Norton Introduction to Literature*, and many other journals and anthologies. He lives in Portland, Oregon, and teaches for Literary Arts and Mountain Writers Series in Portland and for the Lighthouse Writers Workshop in Denver, Colorado. His most recent book is *The Dharma of Poetry: How Poems Can Deepen Your Spiritual Practice and Open You to Joy*.

What to Read Next
from Wisdom Publications

The Dharma of Poetry
How Poems Can Deepen Your Spiritual Practice and Open You to Joy
John Brehm

"John Brehm has done a masterful job in reminding us of the power of our own poetic sensibilities."—Joseph Goldstein, author of *The Experience of Insight*

Zen Master Poems
Dick Allen

"In the tradition of Mary Oliver and David Whyte, Dick Allen's *Zen Master Poems* offers spiritual insights in lucid, seemingly effortless verse."—*Tricycle*

The Clouds Should Know Me by Now
Buddhist Poet Monks of China
Mike O'Connor, Red Pine, and Andrew Schelling

"Here is a breathtaking millennium of Buddhist poet-monks."—*Inquiring Mind*

The Wisdom Anthology of North American Buddhist Poetry
Andrew Schelling

"Erudite, up-to-the-moment, delightful, diverse."
—*Buddhadharma*

Daily Doses of Wisdom
A Year of Buddhist Inspiration
Josh Bartok

"100% organic healing Dharma. Effective for major and minor ailments of the heart."—Kate Wheeler, editor of *The State of Mind Called Beautiful*